DATE DUE

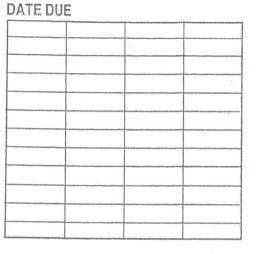

DEMCO

PERCY BYSSHE SHELLEY

Selected
Poems

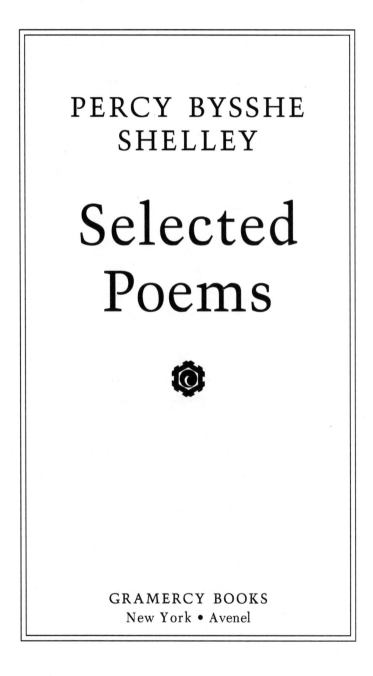

PERCY BYSSHE SHELLEY

Selected Poems

GRAMERCY BOOKS
New York • Avenel

Introduction and compilation
Copyright © 1994 by Random House Value Publishing, Inc.
All rights reserved

This 1994 edition is published by Gramercy Books,
distributed by Random House Value Publishing, Inc.,
40 Engelhard Avenue,
Avenel, New Jersey 07001.

Random House
New York • Toronto • London • Sydney • Auckland

Printed and bound in the United States

Library of Congress Cataloging-in-Publication Data

Shelley, Percy Bysshe 1792-1822
[Selections.]
Percy Bysshe Shelley : selected poems
p.   cm.
ISBN: 0-517-11831-9
I. Title.
PR5403   1994
821'.7—DC20   94-14796   CIP

8 7 6 5 4 3 2

CONTENTS

Alastor

Julian and Maddalo

From Prometheus Unbound

Epipsychidion

Adonais

The Triumph of Life

INTRODUCTION

Percy Bysshe Shelley was a nonconformist who came from the extremely traditional background of the English landed gentry. His grandfather, Sir Bysshe Shelley, was the wealthiest man in Horsham, Sussex, where Shelley was born on August 4, 1792. His father, Timothy Shelley, was a Conservative member of Parliament. Young Percy was in line for a baronetcy and as befitted a young man of his station he was sent to Eton at the age of twelve. It was at this exclusive school that the first signs of his rebelliousness emerged. He openly defied the school's traditional—but cruel—hazing system, as well as the petty tyranny of the schoolmasters. This marked the beginning of his lifelong battle against any form of enslavement and injustice.

When he was eighteen years old, Shelley entered Oxford. But he remained there for only five months. In collaboration with his closest friend, Thomas Jefferson Hogg, he published an anonymous pamphlet entitled *The Necessity of Atheism*, in which it was claimed that the existence of God cannot be proved empirically. When the school authorities discovered the identities of the authors, Shelley and Hogg refused to repudiate their work, and, to their amazement, were expelled.

As Shelley himself noted, he had "a passion for reforming the world," and after his expulsion he moved to London, where he became involved in the radical movements of the day and began writing such political pamphlets as *An Address to the Irish People* and *Declaration of Rights*, both published in 1812. While he was in London, he met Harriet Westbrook, the daughter of a wealthy tavern keeper. Shelley believed that her father had "persecuted her in a most horrible way endeavoring her to go to school." He and the sixteen-year-old girl eloped to Edinburgh, where they were married. Within the year their daughter, Ianthe, was born.

Shelley soon became a disciple of William Godwin, one of the most important radical philosophers of the day and the author of the influential *Inquiry Concerning Political Justice*. He soon fell in love with Godwin's beautiful daughter Mary, whose mother, Mary

Wollstonecraft, was the great English feminist who wrote *Vindication of the Rights of Women*. On July 27, 1814, Shelley left Harriet, who was pregnant with their second child, Charles, and went with Mary to France.

For his time, Shelley held rather liberal views of love and marriage. He believed, for example, that it was immoral to remain married to a person one no longer loved. But he also believed in nonexclusive love and invited Harriet to live with him and Mary, like a sister, an offer Harriet refused. When Shelley and Mary returned from France the following September, they found themselves ostracized by their friends and families. Mary's father—despite his professed liberal views on marriage and Shelley's generosity in taking over his sizable debts—was outraged by the "illicit" relationship. Things were made worse when Harriet, in despair because she was pregnant by an unknown lover, committed suicide in 1816. Soon afterward Shelley and Mary married, in part to help him to get custody of Ianthe and Charles, but after a bitter dispute, the courts ruled Shelley unfit as a father and refused him custody.

Shelley spent the rest of his life in Europe wandering from place to place in self-imposed exile. In 1818, he and Mary moved to Italy. The death of their two young children, Clara and William, which Mary blamed on their incessant traveling, put a strain on their relationship and cast a pall over their marriage, despite the birth of another son, Percy Florence, in 1819.

In 1820 the couple settled in Pisa. Before long a number of their friends—the "Pisan Circle"—gathered around them. The group included, for a time, the poet Lord Byron; Edward Williams, a retired cavalry officer; and his lover, Jane—to whom some of Shelley's last and very romantic poems are addressed.

On July 8, 1822, after a visit with Byron, Shelley and his friend Williams were sailing back Leghorn when a bad storm came upon them and they were both drowned. Their bodies washed up on shore several days later. Shelley's ashes were buried in the Protestant Cemetery at Rome, near the grave of John Keats.

A few days before he died, Shelley said, "If I die tomorrow, I shall have lived to be older than my grandfather; I am ninety years old." In his brief thirty years, he lived a life marked by emotional turmoil and tragedy. An exile from his own land, he had virtually no audience for his poetry.

The appreciation of Shelley's poetry, in his lifetime and afterward, was clouded by his personal life. Robert Southey, England's poet laureate, wrote of Shelley: "With all his genius (and I think *most* highly of it), he was a base, bad man." Thomas Carlyle wrote that Shelley was "weak in genius, weak in character (for these two always go together); a poor thin, spasmodic, hectic, shrill, and pallid being. . . ." The poet Charles Lamb said, "No one was ever the wiser or better for reading Shelley." But Shelley's friend Byron wrote: "You were all brutally mistaken about Shelley, who was, without exception, the *best* and least selfish man I ever knew. I never knew one who was not a beast in comparison." From all accounts, Shelley was, to his friends, a most generous and giving man. As his friend Edward Trelawney wrote: "To know an author personally is too often but to destroy the illusion created by his works . . . Shelley was a grand exception to this rule. To form a just idea of his poetry, you should have witnessed his daily life. . . . The truth was, Shelley loved everything better than himself."

At the center of the continuing controversy surrounding Shelley is "his immoral and decadent relationships" with women, rather than anything he wrote. He was an idealist and his conception of romantic love was extremely quixotic and clearly unrealistic. He believed the perfect mate was one's "antitype" who corresponded to one's intellect and imagination, a kind of mirror image. There is more than a hint of narcissism in his definition of passionate love:

> If we reason, we would be understood, if we imagine, we would that the airy children of our brain were born anew within another's; if we feel, we would that another's nerves should vibrate to our own, that the beams of their eyes should kindle at once and mix and melt into our own, that lips of motionless ice should not reply to lips quivering and burning with the heart's best blood. This is Love.

But Shelley acknowledged the limitations of searching for perfection: "I think one is always in love with something or other; the error, and I confess it is not easy for spirits cased in flesh and blood to avoid it, consists in seeking in a mortal image the likeness of what is perhaps eternal." Shelley clearly dramatizes this in his poem *Alastor*, in which a youth searches for his ideal vision of beauty and goes to his death unfulfilled. The story parallels Shelley's own life, in which none of the women compared to his ideal, even Mary, who probably suffered the most from his ceaseless search for his "antitype." *Epipsychidion*, one of Shelley's most passionate and romantic poems, is addressed to Emilia Viviani, the nineteen-year-old daughter of the governor of Pisa, who at her father's instigation was incarcerated in a convent. At the end of the poem, the twenty-nine-year-old Shelley urges her to run away with him. In real life she yielded to a marriage arranged by her father and was soon asking Shelley for money, a predicament about which Mary cuttingly commented, "So much for Percy's platonics."

If his idealism caused confusion in his personal life, it was the essential source of his visionary poetry. His verse was fueled by a qualified optimism and his conviction that he could help reform the world through his writing. He wrote: "The great instrument of moral good is the imagination."

In *A Defense of Poetry*, Shelley stated that poetry is "the very image of life expressed in its eternal truth," something "divine . . . at once the center and circumference of knowledge." The effect of poetry, he believed, was that "it awakens and enlarges the mind," lifting "the veil from the hidden beauty of the world," revealing some metaphysical truth. Shelley thought that love is the source of power for change. He wrote, "The great secret of morals is Love," which he defines as the identification with a "thought, action, or person, not our own," where one becomes moral through the means of empathizing. This belief is at the core of *Prometheus Unbound*, the drama that is considered his masterpiece. W. B. Yeats, the great Irish poet, called it one of "the sacred books of the world." In the work, the mythic Titan Prometheus—who has been chained to a rock by Jupiter for giving humanity the gift of fire—is freed only when he truly understands and stops hating his oppressor. Shelley's point was that the source of evil and despotism in the world is man himself not some outside force, and that only through love and constant vigilance can mankind permanently overcome tyranny.

Although because of his personal life there is continued interest in Shelley outside his verse, his poetry lives on because of its genuine merits. William Wordsworth, the great Romantic poet, paid him this compliment: "Shelley is one of the best *artists* of us all: I mean in workmanship of style." Indeed Shelley's greatest poems aspire to the highest ideals of humanity and remain some of Romanticism's most distinguished achievements.

Collected in this volume are Shelley's finest, as well as his most popular, works. Selected from his shorter lyric poems are such favorites as "Mont Blanc," "Mutability," and "Ozymandias." Included from his longer works are excerpts from *Prometheus Unbound*, as well as the entire texts of *Epipsychidion*; *Adonais*; and *The Triumph of Life*, which was left incomplete at the time of his death.

CHRISTOPHER MOORE

New York
1994

Lyric Poems

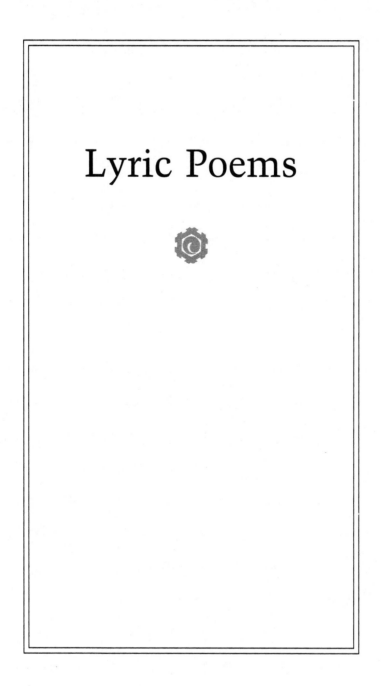

MUTABILITY

We are as clouds that veil the midnight moon;
   How restlessly they speed, and gleam, and quiver,
Streaking the darkness radiantly!—yet soon
   Night closes round, and they are lost forever:

Or like forgotten lyres, whose dissonant strings
   Give various response to each varying blast,
To whose frail frame no second motion brings
   One mood or modulation like the last.

We rest—A dream has power to poison sleep;
   We rise—One wandering thought pollutes the day;
We feel, conceive or reason, laugh or weep;
   Embrace fond woe, or cast our cares away:

It is the same!—For, be it joy or sorrow,
   The path of its departure still is free:
Man's yesterday may ne'er be like his morrow;
   Naught may endure but Mutability.

TO ——

Oh! there are spirits of the air,
  And genii of the evening breeze,
And gentle ghosts, with eyes as fair
  As star-beams among twilight trees—
Such lovely ministers to meet
Oft hast thou turned from men thy lonely feet.

With mountain winds, and babbling springs,
  And moonlight seas, that are the voice
Of these inexplicable things,
  Thou didst hold commune, and rejoice
When they did answer thee; but they
Cast, like a worthless boon, thy love away.

And thou hast sought in starry eyes
  Beams that were never meant for thine,
Another's wealth—tame sacrifice
  To a fond faith! still dost thou pine?
Still dost thou hope that greeting hands,
Voice, looks, or lips, may answer thy demands?

Ah! wherefore didst thou build thine hope
  On the false earth's inconstancy?
Did thine own mind afford no scope
  Of love, or moving thoughts to thee?
That natural scenes or human smiles
Could steal the power to wind thee in their wiles

Yes, all the faithless smiles are fled
  Whose falsehood left thee brokenhearted;
The glory of the moon is dead;

Night's ghosts and dreams have now departed;
Thine own soul still is true to thee,
But changed to a foul fiend through misery.

This fiend, whose ghastly presence ever
    Beside thee like thy shadow hangs,
Dream not to chase—the mad endeavor
    Would scourge thee to severer pangs.
Be as thou art. Thy settled fate,
Dark as it is, all change would aggravate.

TO WORDSWORTH

Poet of Nature, thou hast wept to know
That things depart which never may return:
Childhood and youth, friendship and love's first glow,
Have fled like sweet dreams, leaving thee to mourn.
These common woes I feel. One loss is mine
Which thou too feel'st, yet I alone deplore.
Thou wert as a lone star, whose light did shine
On some frail bark in winter's midnight roar:
Thou hast like to a rock-built refuge stood
Above the blind and battling multitude:
In honored poverty thy voice did weave
Songs consecrate to truth and liberty—
Deserting these, thou leavest me to grieve,
Thus having been, that thou shouldst cease to be.

FEELINGS OF A REPUBLICAN ON THE FALL OF BONAPARTE

I hated thee, fallen tyrant! I did groan
To think that a most unambitious slave,
Like thou, shouldst dance and revel on the grave
Of Liberty. Thou mightst have built thy throne
Where it had stood even now: thou didst prefer
A frail and bloody pomp which Time has swept
In fragments towards Oblivion. Massacre,
For this I prayed, would on thy sleep have crept,
Treason and Slavery, Rapine, Fear, and Lust,
And stifled thee, their minister. I know
Too late, since thou and France are in the dust,
That Virtue owns a more eternal foe
Than Force or Fraud: old Custom, legal Crime,
And bloody Faith the foulest birth of Time.

LINES

I

The cold earth slept below,
    Above the cold sky shone;
And all around, with a chilling sound,
    From caves of ice and fields of snow,
    The breath of night like death did flow
      Beneath the sinking moon.

II

The wintry hedge was black,
    The green grass was not seen,
The birds did rest on the bare thorn's breast,
    Whose roots, beside the pathway track,
    Had bound their folds o'er many a crack
      Which the frost had made between.

III

Thine eyes glowed in the glare
    Of the moon's dying light;
As a fen-fire's beam on a sluggish stream
    Gleams dimly, so the moon shone there,
    And it yellowed the swings of thy raven hair,
      That shook in the wind of night.

IV

The moon made thy lips pale, beloved—
    The wind made thy bosom chill—
The night did shed on thy dear head
    Its frozen dew, and thou didst lie
    Where the bitter breath of the naked sky
      Might visit thee at will.

HYMN TO INTELLECTUAL BEAUTY

I

The awful shadow of some unseen Power
   Floats though unseen amongst us—visiting
   This various world with as inconstant wing
   As summer winds that creep from flower to flower—
Like moonbeams that behind some piney mountain shower,
   It visits with inconstant glance
   Each human heart and countenance;
Like hues and harmonies of evening—
   Like clouds in starlight widely spread—
   Like memory of music fled—
   Like aught that for its grace may be
Dear, and yet dearer for its mystery.

II

Spirit of BEAUTY, that dost consecrate
   With thine own hues all thou dost shine upon
   Of human thought or form—where art thou gone?
Why dost thou pass away and leave our state,
This dim vast vale of tears, vacant and desolate?
   Ask why the sunlight not forever
   Weaves rainbows o'er yon mountain river,
Why aught should fail and fade that once is shown,
   Why fear and dream and death and birth
   Cast on the daylight of this earth
   Such gloom—why man has such a scope
For love and hate, despondency and hope?

III

No voice from some sublimer world hath ever
   To sage or poet these responses given—

Therefore the name of God and ghosts and Heaven,
Remain the records of their vain endeavor,
Frail spells—whose uttered charm might not avail to sever,
   From all we hear and all we see,
   Doubt, chance, and mutability.
Thy light alone—like mist o'er mountains driven,
   Or music by the night wind sent
   Through strings of some still instrument,
   Or moonlight on a midnight stream,
Gives grace and truth to life's unquiet dream.

IV

Love, Hope, and Self-esteem, like clouds depart
   And come, for some uncertain moments lent.
   Man were immortal, and omnipotent,
Didst thou, unknown and awful as thou art,
Keep with thy glorious train firm state within his heart.
   Thou messenger of sympathies,
   That wax and wane in lovers' eyes—
Thou—that to human thought art nourishment,
   Like darkness to a dying flame!
   Depart not as thy shadow came,
   Depart not—lest the grave should be,
Like life and fear, a dark reality.

V

While yet a boy I sought for ghosts, and sped
   Through many a listening chamber, cave and ruin,
   And starlight wood, with fearful steps pursuing
Hopes of high talk with the departed dead.
I called on poisonous names with which our youth is fed;
   I was not heard—I saw them not—
   When musing deeply on the lot
Of life, at that sweet time when winds are wooing
   All vital things that wake to bring
   News of buds and blossoming—

Sudden, thy shadow fell on me;
I shrieked, and clasped my hands in ecstasy!

VI

I vowed that I would dedicate my powers
  To thee and thine—have I not kept the vow?
  With beating heart and streaming eyes, even now
I call the phantoms of a thousand hours
Each from his voiceless grave: they have in visioned
    bowers
  Of studious zeal or love's delight
  Outwatched with me the envious night—
They know that never joy illumed my brow
  Unlinked with hope that thou wouldst free
  This world from its dark slavery,
  That thou—O awful LOVELINESS,
Wouldst give whate'er these words cannot express.

VII

The day becomes more solemn and serene
  When noon is past—there is a harmony
  In autumn, and a luster in its sky,
Which through the summer is not heard or seen,
As if it could not be, as if it had not been!
  Thus let thy power, which like the truth
  Of nature on my passive youth
Descended, to my onward life supply
  Its calm—to one who worships thee,
  And every form containing thee,
  Whom, SPIRIT fair, thy spells did bind
To fear himself, and love all human kind.

MONT BLANC

Lines Written in the Vale of Chamouni

I

The everlasting universe of things
Flows through the mind, and rolls its rapid waves,
Now dark—now glittering—now reflecting gloom—
Now lending splendor, where from secret springs
The source of human thought its tribute brings
Of waters—with a sound but half its own.
Such as a feeble brook will oft assume
In the wild woods, among the mountains lone,
Where waterfalls around it leap forever,
Where woods and winds contend, and a vast river
Over its rocks ceaselessly bursts and raves.

II

Thus thou, Ravine of Arve—dark, deep Ravine—
Thou many-colored, many-voiced vale,
Over whose pines, and crags, and caverns sail
Fast cloud shadows and sunbeams: awful scene,
Where Power in likeness of the Arve comes down
From the ice gulfs that gird his secret throne,
Bursting through these dark mountains like the flame
Of lightning through the tempest—thou dost lie,
Thy giant brood of pines around thee clinging,
Children of elder time, in whose devotion
The chainless winds still come and ever came
To drink their odors, and their mighty swinging
To hear—an old and solemn harmony;
Thine earthly rainbows stretched across the sweep
Of the ethereal waterfall, whose veil

Robes some unsculptured image, the strange sleep
Which when the voices of the desert fail
Wraps all in its own deep eternity—
Thy caverns echoing to the Arve's commotion,
A loud, lone sound no other sound can tame;
Thou art pervaded with that ceaseless motion,
Thou art the path of that unresting sound—
Dizzy Ravine! and when I gaze on thee
I seem as in a trance sublime and strange
To muse on my own separate fantasy,
My own, my human mind, which passively
Now renders and receives fast influencings,
Holding an unremitting interchange
With the clear universe of things around;
One legion of wild thoughts, whose wandering wings
Now float above thy darkness, and now rest
Where that or thou art no unbidden guest,
In the still cave of the witch Poesy,
Seeking among the shadows that pass by
Ghosts of all things that are, some shade of thee,
Some phantom, some faint image; till the breast
From which they fled recalls them, thou art there!

III

Some say that gleams of a remoter world
Visit the soul in sleep—that death is slumber,
And that its shapes the busy thoughts outnumber
Of those who wake and live—I look on high;
Has some unknown omnipotence unfurled
The veil of life and death? or do I lie
In dream, and does the mightier world of sleep
Spread far around and inaccessibly
Its circles? For the very spirit fails,
Driven like a homeless cloud from steep to steep
That vanishes among the viewless gales!
Far, far above, piercing the infinite sky,

Mont Blanc appears—still, snowy, and serene—
Its subject mountains their unearthly forms
Pile around it, ice and rock; broad vales between
Of frozen floods, unfathomable deeps,
Blue as the overhanging heaven, that spread
And wind among the accumulated steeps;
A desert peopled by the storms alone,
Save when the eagle brings some hunter's bone,
And the wolf tracks her there—how hideously
Its shapes are heaped around! rude, bare, and high,
Ghastly, and scarred, and riven—Is this the scene
Where the old Earthquake-daemon taught her young
Ruin? Were these their toys? or did a sea
Of fire, envelope once this silent snow?
None can reply—all seems eternal now.
The wilderness has a mysterious tongue
Which teaches awful doubt, or faith so mild,
So solemn, so serene, that man may be
But for such faith with nature reconciled,
Thou hast a voice, great Mountain, to repeal
Large codes of fraud and woe; not understood
By all, but which the wise, and great, and good
Interpret, or make felt, or deeply feel.

IV

The fields, the lakes, the forests, and the streams,
Ocean, and all the living things that dwell
Within the daedal earth; lightning, and rain,
Earthquake, and fiery flood, and hurricane,
The torpor of the year when feeble dreams
Visit the hidden buds, or dreamless sleep
Holds every future leaf and flower—the bound
With which from that detested trance they leap;
The works and ways of man, their death and birth,
And that of him and all that his may be;
All things that move and breathe with toil and sound

Are born and die; revolve, subside and swell.
Power dwells apart in its tranquility
Remote, serene, and inaccessible:
And *this*, the naked countenance of earth,
On which I gaze, even these primeval mountains
Teach the adverting mind. The glaciers creep
Like snakes that watch their prey, from their far fountains,
Slow rolling on; there, many a precipice,
Frost and the Sun in scorn of mortal power
Have piled: dome, pyramid, and pinnacle,
A city of death, distinct with many a tower
And wall impregnable of beaming ice.
Yet not a city, but a flood of ruin
Is there, that from the boundaries of the sky
Rolls its perpetual stream; vast pines are strewing
Its destined path, or in the mangled soil
Branchless and shattered stand: the rocks, drawn down
From yon remotest waste, have overthrown
The limits of the dead and living world,
Never to be reclaimed. The dwelling place
Of insects, beasts, and birds, becomes its spoil;
Their food and their retreat forever gone,
So much of life and joy is lost. The race
Of man, flies far in dread; his work and dwelling
Vanish, like smoke before the tempest's stream,
And their place is not known. Below, vast caves
Shine in the rushing torrents' restless gleam,
Which from those secret chasms in tumult welling
Meet in the vale, and one majestic River,
The breath and blood of distant lands, forever
Rolls its loud waters to the ocean waves,
Breathes its swift vapors to the circling air.

v

Mont Blanc yet gleams on high—the power is there,
The still and solemn power of many sights,

And many sounds, and much of life and death.
In the calm darkness of the moonless nights,
In the lone glare of day, the snows descend
Upon that Mountain; none beholds them there,
Nor when the flakes burn in the sinking sun,
Or the star-beams dart through them—Winds contend
Silently there, and heap the snow with breath
Rapid and strong, but silently! Its home
The voiceless lightning in these solitudes
Keeps innocently, and like vapor broods
Over the snow. The secret strength of things
Which governs thought, and to the infinite dome
Of heaven is as a law, inhabits thee!
And what were thou, and earth, and stars, and sea,
If to the human mind's imaginings
Silence and solitude were vacancy?

TO CONSTANTIA

Thy voice, slow rising like a Spirit, lingers
O'ershadowing me with soft and lulling wings;
The blood and life within thy snowy fingers
Teach witchcraft to the instrumental strings.
    My brain is wild, my breath comes quick,
    The blood is listening in my frame,
    And thronging shadows fast and thick
    Fall on my overflowing eyes,
    My heart is quivering like a flame;
As morning dew, that in the sunbeam dies,
I am dissolved in these consuming ecstasies.

I have no life, Constantia, but in thee;
Whilst, like the world-surrounding air, thy song
Flows on, and fills all things with melody:
Now is thy voice a tempest, swift and strong,
    On which, as one in trance upborne,
    Secure o'er woods and waves I sweep
    Rejoicing, like a cloud of morn:
    Now 'tis the breath of summer's night
    Which, where the starry waters sleep
Round western isles with incense blossoms bright,
Lingering, suspends my soul in its voluptuous flight.

A deep and breathless awe, like the swift change
Of dreams unseen, but felt in youthful slumbers;
Wild, sweet, yet incommunicably strange,
Thou breathest now, in fast ascending numbers:
    The cope of Heaven seems rent and cloven
    By the enchantment of thy strain,
    And o'er my shoulders wings are woven

To follow its sublime career,
Beyond the mighty moons that wane
Upon the verge of Nature's utmost sphere,
Till the world's shadowy walls are past, and disappear.

Cease, cease—for such wild lessons madmen learn:
Long thus to sink—thus to be lost and die
Perhaps is death indeed—Constantia turn!
Yes! in thine eyes a power like light doth lie,
Even though the sounds, its voice, that were
Between thy lips are laid to sleep
Within thy breath and on thy hair
Like odor it is lingering yet—
And from thy touch like fire doth leap:
Even while I write my burning cheeks are wet—
Such things the heart can feel and learn, but not forget!

OZYMANDIAS

I met a traveler from an antique land,
Who said—"Two vast and trunkless legs of stone
Stand in the desert . . . . Near them, on the sand,
Half sunk a shattered visage lies, whose frown,
And wrinkled lip, and sneer of cold command,
Tell that its sculptor well those passions read
Which yet survive, stamped on these lifeless things,
The hand that mocked them, and the heart that fed;
And on the pedestal, these words appear:
My name is Ozymandias, King of Kings,
Look on my Works, ye Mighty, and despair!
Nothing beside remains. Round the decay
Of that colossal Wreck, boundless and bare
The lone and level sands stretch far away."

ON A FADED VIOLET

I

The odor from the flower is gone;
　　Which like thy kisses breathed on me;
The color from the flower is flown
　　Which glowed of thee and only thee!

II

A shriveled, lifeless, vacant form,
　　It lies on my abandoned breast,
And mocks the heart which yet is warm,
　　With cold and silent rest.

III

I weep—my tears revive it not!
　　I sigh—it breathes no more on me;
Its mute and uncomplaining lot
　　Is such as mine should be.

STANZAS WRITTEN IN DEJECTION—

DECEMBER 1818, NEAR NAPLES

The Sun is warm, the sky is clear,
The waves are dancing fast and bright,
Blue isles and snowy mountains wear
The purple noon's transparent might,
The breath of the moist earth is light
Around its unexpanded buds;
Like many a voice of one delight
The winds, the birds, the Ocean floods;
The City's voice itself is soft, like Solitude's.

I see the Deep's untrampled floor
With green and purple seaweeds strown;
I see the waves upon the shore
Like light dissolved in star-showers, thrown;
I sit upon the sands alone;
The lightning of the noontide Ocean
Is flashing round me, and a tone
Arises from its measured motion,
How sweet! did any heart now share in my emotion.

Alas, I have nor hope nor health
Nor peace within nor calm around,
Nor that content surpassing wealth
The sage in meditation found,
And walked with inward glory crowned;
Nor fame nor power nor love nor leisure—
Others I see whom these surround,
Smiling they live and call life pleasure:
To me that cup has been dealt in another measure.

Yet now despair itself is mild,
Even as the winds and waters are;
I could lie down like a tired child
And weep away the life of care
Which I have borne and yet must bear
Till Death like Sleep might steal on me,
And I might feel in the warm air
My cheek grow cold, and hear the Sea
Breathe o'er my dying brain its last monotony.

Some might lament that I were cold,
As I, when this sweet day is gone,
Which my lost heart, too soon grown old,
Insults with this untimely moan—
They might lament—for I am one
Whom men love not, and yet regret;
Unlike this day, which, when the Sun
Shall on its stainless glory set,
Will linger though enjoyed, like joy in Memory yet.

SONNET

Lift not the painted veil which those who live
Call Life; though unreal shapes be pictured there
And it but mimic all we would believe
With colors idly spread—behind, lurk Fear
And Hope, twin Destinies, who ever weave
Their shadows o'er the chasm, sightless and drear.
I knew one who had lifted it . . . . he sought,
For his lost heart was tender, things to love
But found them not, alas; nor was there aught
The world contains, the which he could approve.
Through the unheeding many he did move,
A splendor among shadows—a bright blot
Upon this gloomy scene—a Spirit that strove
For truth, and like the Preacher, found it not—

SONNET

Ye hasten to the grave! What seek ye there,
Ye restless thoughts, and busy purposes
Of the idle brain, which the world's livery wear?
O thou quick Heart, which pantest to possess
All that pale Expectation feigneth fair!
Thou vainly curious mind which wouldest guess
Whence thou didst come, and whither thou must go,
And all that never yet was known, would know,
O whither hasten ye, that thus ye press,
With such swift feet life's green and pleasant path,
Seeking alike from happiness and woe
A refuge in the cavern of gray death?
O Heart and Mind and Thoughts what thing do you
Hope to inherit in the grave below?

SONG TO THE MEN OF ENGLAND

Men of England, wherefore plow
For the lords who lay ye low?
Wherefore weave with toil and care
The rich robes your tyrants wear?

Wherefore feed and clothe and save
From the cradle to the grave
Those ungrateful drones who would
Drain your sweat—nay, drink your blood?

Wherefore, Bees of England, forge
Many a weapon, chain, and scourge,
That these stingless drones may spoil
The forced produce of your toil?

Have ye leisure, comfort, calm,
Shelter, food, love's gentle balm?
Or what is it ye buy so dear
With your pain and with your fear?

The seed ye sow, another reaps;
The wealth ye find, another keeps;
The robes ye weave, another wears;
The arms ye forge, another bears.

Sow seed—but let no tyrant reap:
Find wealth—let no impostor heap:
Weave robes—let not the idle wear:
Forge arms—in your defense to bear.

Shrink to your cellars, holes, and cells—
In halls ye deck another dwells.

Why shake the chains ye wrought? when see
The steel ye tempered glance on ye.

With plow and spade and hoe and loom
Trace your grave and build your tomb
And weave your winding sheet—till fair
England be your Sepulcher.

ENGLAND IN 1819

An old, mad, blind, despised, and dying King;
Princes, the dregs of their dull race, who flow
Through public scorn—mud from a muddy spring:
Rulers who neither see nor feel nor know,
But leechlike to their fainting country cling
Till they drop, blind in blood, without a blow.
A people starved and stabbed in th'untilled field;
An army, whom liberticide and prey
Makes as a two-edged sword to all who wield;
Golden and sanguine laws which tempt and slay:
Religion Christless, Godless—a book sealed;
A senate, Time's worst statute, unrepealed—
Are graves from which a glorious Phantom may
Burst, to illumine our tempestuous day.

TO SIDMOUTH AND CASTLEREAGH

As from their ancestral oak
   Two empty ravens wind their clarion,
Yell by yell, and croak by croak,
When they scent the noonday smoke
   Of fresh human carrion—

As two gibbering nightbirds flit
   From their bowers of deadly yew
Through the night to frighten it—
When the moon is in a fit,
   And the stars are none, or few—

As a shark and dogfish wait
   Under an Atlantic isle
For the Negro ship, whose freight
Is the theme of their debate,
   Wrinkling their red gills the while—

Are ye—two vultures sick for battle,
   Two scorpions under one wet stone,
Two bloodless wolves whose dry throats rattle,
Two crows perched on the murrained cattle,
   Two vipers tangled into one.

ODE TO THE WEST WIND

I

O wild West Wind, thou breath of Autumn's being,
Thou, from whose unseen presence the leaves dead
Are driven, like ghosts from an enchanter fleeing,

Yellow, and black, and pale, and hectic red,
Pestilence-stricken multitudes: O Thou,
Who chariotest to their dark wintry bed

The winged seeds, where they lie cold and low,
Each like a corpse within its grave, until
Thine azure sister of the Spring shall blow

Her clarion o'er the dreaming earth, and fill
(Driving sweet buds like flocks to feed in air)
With living hues and odors plain and hill:

Wild Spirit, which art moving everywhere;
Destroyer and Preserver; hear, O hear!

II

Thou on whose stream, 'mid the steep sky's commotion,
Loose clouds like Earth's decaying leaves are shed,
Shook from the tangled boughs of Heaven and Ocean,

Angels of rain and lightning: there are spread
On the blue surface of thine aery surge,
Like the bright hair uplifted from the head

Of some fierce Maenad, even from the dim verge
Of the horizon to the zenith's height,
The locks of the approaching storm. Thou Dirge

Of the dying year, to which this closing night
Will be the dome of a vast sepulcher,
Vaulted with all thy congregated might

Of vapors, from whose solid atmosphere
Black rain and fire and hail will burst: O hear!

III

Thou who didst waken from his summer dreams
The blue Mediterranean, where he lay,
Lulled by the coil of his crystalline streams,

Beside a pumice isle in Baiae's bay,
And saw in sleep old palaces and towers
Quivering within the wave's intenser day,

All overgrown with azure moss and flowers
So sweet, the sense faints picturing them! Thou
For whose path the Atlantic's level powers

Cleave themselves into chasms, while far below
The sea-blooms and the oozy woods which wear
The sapless foliage of the ocean, know

Thy voice, and suddenly grow gray with fear,
And tremble and despoil themselves: O hear!

IV

If I were a dead leaf thou mightest bear;
If I were a swift cloud to fly with thee;
A wave to pant beneath thy power, and share

The impulse of thy strength, only less free
Than thou, O Uncontrollable! If even
I were as in my boyhood, and could be

The comrade of thy wanderings over Heaven,
As then, when to outstrip thy skiey speed
Scarce seemed a vision; I would ne'er have striven

As thus with thee in prayer in my sore need.
Oh! lift me as a wave, a leaf, a cloud!
I fall upon the thorns of life! I bleed!

A heavy weight of hours has chained and bowed
One too like thee: tameless, and swift, and proud.

V

Make me thy lyre, even as the forest is:
What if my leaves are falling like its own!
The tumult of thy mighty harmonies

Will take from both a deep, autumnal tone,
Sweet though in sadness. Be thou, Spirit fierce,
My spirit! Be thou me, impetuous one!

Drive my dead thoughts over the universe
Like withered leaves to quicken a new birth!
And, by the incantation of this verse,

Scatter, as from an unextinguished hearth
Ashes and sparks, my words among mankind!
Be through my lips to unawakened Earth

The trumpet of a prophecy! O Wind,
If Winter comes, can Spring be far behind?

THE INDIAN GIRL'S SONG

I arise from dreams of thee
In the first sleep of night—
The winds are breathing low
And the stars are burning bright.
I arise from dreams of thee—
And a spirit in my feet
Has borne me—Who knows how?
To thy chamber window, sweet!—

The wandering airs they faint
On the dark silent stream—
The champak odors fail
Like sweet thoughts in a dream;
The nightingale's complaint—
It dies upon her heart—
As I must die on thine
O beloved as thou art!

O lift me from the grass!
I die, I faint, I fail!
Let thy love in kisses rain
On my lips and eyelids pale.
My cheek is cold and white, alas!
My heart beats loud and fast.
Oh press it close to thine again
Where it will break at last.

LOVE'S PHILOSOPHY

I

The fountains mingle with the river
   And the rivers with the Ocean,
The winds of Heaven mix forever
   With a sweet emotion;
Nothing in the world is single;
   All things by a law divine
In one spirit meet and mingle.
   Why not I with thine?—

II

See the mountains kiss high Heaven
   And the waves clasp one another;
No sister-flower would be forgiven
   If it disdained its brother;
And the sunlight clasps the earth
   And the moonbeams kiss the sea:
What is all this sweet work worth
   If thou kiss not me?

THE CLOUD

I bring fresh showers for the thirsting flowers,
    From the seas and the streams;
I bear light shade for the leaves when laid
    In their noonday dreams.
From my wings are shaken the dews that waken
    The sweet buds every one,
When rocked to rest on their mother's breast,
    As she dances about the Sun.
I wield the flail of the lashing hail,
    And whiten the green plains under,
And then again I dissolve it in rain,
    And laugh as I pass in thunder.

I sift the snow on the mountains below,
    And their great pines groan aghast;
And all the night 'tis my pillow white,
    While I sleep in the arms of the blast.
Sublime on the towers of my skiey bowers,
    Lightning my pilot sits;
In a cavern under is fettered the thunder,
    It struggles and howls at fits;
Over Earth and Ocean, with gentle motion,
    This pilot is guiding me,
Lured by the love of the genii that move
    In the depths of the purple sea;
Over the rills, and the crags, and the hills,
    Over the lakes and the plains,
Wherever he dream, under mountain or stream,
    The Spirit he loves remains;
And I all the while bask in Heaven's blue smile,
    Whilst he is dissolving in rains.

The sanguine Sunrise, with his meteor eyes,
    And his burning plumes outspread,
Leaps on the back of my sailing rack,
    When the morning star shines dead;
As on the jag of a mountain crag,
    Which an earthquake rocks and swings,

An eagle alit one moment may sit
    In the light of its golden wings.
And when Sunset may breathe, from the lit Sea beneath,
    Its ardors of rest and of love,
And the crimson pall of eve may fall
    From the depth of Heaven above,
With wings folded I rest, on mine aery nest,
    As still as a brooding dove.

That orbed maiden with white fire laden
    Whom mortals call the Moon,
Glides glimmering o'er my fleecelike floor,
    By the midnight breezes strewn;
And wherever the beat of her unseen feet,
    Which only the angels hear,
May have broken the woof, of my tent's thin roof,
    The stars peep behind her, and peer;
And I laugh to see them whirl and flee,
    Like a swarm of golden bees,
When I widen the rent in my wind-built tent,
    Till the calm rivers, lakes, and seas,
Like strips of the sky fallen through me on high,
    Are each paved with the moon and these.

I bind the Sun's throne with a burning zone
    And the Moon's with a girdle of pearl;
The volcanos are dim and the stars reel and swim
    When the whirlwinds my banner unfurl.
From cape to cape, with a bridgelike shape,

Over a torrent sea,
Sunbeam-proof, I hang like a roof—
    The mountains its columns be!
The triumphal arch, through which I march
    With hurricane, fire, and snow,
When the Powers of the Air, are chained to my chair,
    Is the million-colored Bow;
The sphere-fire above its soft colors wove
    While the moist Earth was laughing below.

I am the daughter of Earth and Water,
    And the nursling of the Sky;
I pass through the pores, of the ocean and shores;
    I change, but I cannot die—
For after the rain, when with never a stain
    The pavilion of Heaven is bare,
And the winds and sunbeams, with their convex gleams,
    Build up the blue dome of Air—
I silently laugh at my own cenotaph,
    And out of the caverns of rain,
Like a child from the womb, like a ghost from the tomb,
    I arise, and unbuild it again.

TO A SKYLARK

Hail to thee, blithe Spirit!
   Bird thou never wert—
That from Heaven, or near it,
   Pourest thy full heart
In profuse strains of unpremeditated art.

Higher still and higher
   From the earth thou springest
Like a cloud of fire;
   The blue deep thou wingest,
And singing still dost soar, and soaring ever singest.

In the golden lightning
   Of the sunken Sun—
O'er which clouds are brightning,
   Thou dost float and run;
Like an unbodied joy whose race is just begun.

The pale purple even
   Melts around thy flight,
Like a star of Heaven
   In the broad daylight
Thou art unseen—but yet I hear thy shrill delight,

Keen as are the arrows
   Of that silver sphere,
Whose intense lamp narrows
   In the white dawn clear
Until we hardly see—we feel that it is there.

All the earth and air
   With thy voice is loud,
As when Night is bare

SONG OF APOLLO

The sleepless Hours who watch me as I lie
  Curtained with star-enwoven tapestries
From the broad moonlight of the open sky;
  Fanning the busy dreams from my dim eyes,
Waken me when their mother, the gray Dawn,
Tells them that Dreams and that the moon is gone.

Then I arise; and climbing Heaven's blue dome,
  I walk over the mountains and the waves,
Leaving my robe upon the Ocean foam.
  My footsteps pave the clouds with fire; the caves
Are filled with my bright presence, and the air
Leaves the green Earth to my embraces bare.

The sunbeams are my shafts with which I kill
  Deceit, that loves the night and fears the day.
All men who do, or even imagine ill
  Fly me; and from the glory of my ray
Good minds, and open actions take new might
Until diminished, by the reign of night.

I feed the clouds, the rainbows and the flowers
  With their ethereal colors; the moon's globe
And the pure stars in their eternal bowers
  Are cinctured with my power as with a robe;
Whatever lamps on Earth or Heaven may shine
Are portions of one spirit; which is mine.

I stand at noon upon the peak of Heaven;
  Then with unwilling steps, I linger down
Into the clouds of the Atlantic even.

From one lonely cloud
The moon rains out her beams—and Heaven is overflowed.

  What thou art we know not;
    What is most like thee?
From rainbow clouds there flow not
    Drops so bright to see
As from thy presence showers a rain of melody.

  Like a Poet hidden
    In the light of thought,
Singing hymns unbidden,
    Till the world is wrought
To sympathy with hopes and fears it heeded not:

  Like a highborn maiden
    In a palace tower,
Soothing her love-laden
    Soul in secret hour,
With music sweet as love—which overflows her bower:

  Like a glowworm golden
    In a dell of dew,
Scattering unbeholden
    Its aerial hue
Among the flowers and grass which screen it from the view:

  Like a rose embowered
    In its own green leaves—
By warm winds deflowered—
    Till the scent it gives
Makes faint with too much sweet these heavy-winged
        thieves:

  Sound of vernal showers
    On the twinkling grass,
Rain-awakened flowers,

All that ever was
Joyous, and clear and fresh, thy music doth surpass.

Teach us, Sprite or Bird,
    What sweet thoughts are thine;
I have never heard
    Praise of love or wine
That panted forth a flood of rapture so divine:

Chorus Hymeneal
    Or triumphal chaunt
Matched with thine would be all
    But an empty vaunt,
A thing wherein we feel there is some hidden want.

What objects are the fountains
    Of thy happy strain?
What fields or waves or mountains?
    What shapes of sky or plain?
What love of thine own kind? what ignorance of pain?

With thy clear keen joyance
    Languor cannot be—
Shadow of annoyance
    Never came near thee;
Thou lovest—but ne'er knew love's sad satiety.

Waking or asleep,
    Thou of death must deem
Things more true and deep
    Than we mortals dream,
Or how could thy notes flow in such a crystal stream?

We look before and after,
    And pine for what is not—
Our sincerest laughter

With some pain is fraught—
Our sweetest songs are those that tell of saddest
        thought.

Yet if we could scorn
    Hate and pride and fear;
If we were things born
    Not to shed a tear,
I know not how thy joy we ever should come near.

Better than all measures
    Of delightful sound—
Better than all treasures
    That in books are found—
Thy skill to poet were, thou Scorner of the groun

Teach me half the gladness
    That thy brain must know,
Such harmonious madness
    From my lips would flow
The world should listen then—as I am listening

For grief that I depart they weep and frown—
What look is more delightful, than the smile
With which I soothe them from the Western isle?

I am the eye with which the Universe
    Beholds itself, and knows it is divine.
All harmony of instrument and verse,
    All prophesy and medicine are mine;
All light of art or nature—to my song
Victory and praise, in its own right, belong.

SONG OF PAN

From the forests and highlands
  We come, we come,
From the river-girt islands
  Where loud waves were dumb
Listening my sweet pipings.
    The wind in the reeds and the rushes,
    The bees on the bells of thyme,
    The birds in the myrtle bushes,
    The cicadae above in the lime,
      And the lizards below in the grass,
Were silent as even old Tmolus was,
    Listening my sweet pipings.

Liquid Peneus was flowing—
  And all dark Tempe lay
In Olympus' shadow, outgrowing
  The light of the dying day,
  Speeded with my sweet pipings.
    The sileni and sylvans and fauns
    And the nymphs of the woods and the waves,
    To the edge of the moist river-lawns
    And the brink of the dewy caves,
      And all that did then attend and follow
Were as silent for love, as you now, Apollo,
    For envy of my sweet pipings.

I sang of the dancing stars,
  I sang of the daedal Earth,
And of Heaven, and the giant wars,
  And Love and Death and Birth;
    And then I changed my pipings,

Singing how, down the vales of Maenalus
I pursued a maiden and clasped a reed.
Gods and men, we are all deluded thus!—
It breaks in our bosom and then we bleed;
    They wept as, I think, both ye now would,
If envy or age had not frozen your blood,
    At the sorrow of my sweet pipings.

TO ——

I

I fear thy kisses, gentle maiden,
    Thou needest not fear mine;
My spirit is too deeply laden
    Ever to burthen thine.

II

I fear thy mien, thy tones, thy motion,
    Thou needest not fear mine;
Innocent is the heart's devotion
    With which I worship thine.

TO THE MOON

I

Art thou pale for weariness
Of climbing heaven and gazing on the earth,
　Wandering companionless
Among the stars that have a different birth—
And ever changing, like a joyless eye
That finds no object worth its constancy?

II

　Thou chosen sister of the Spirit,
That gazes on thee till in thee it pities . . .

FRAGMENT: THE WANING MOON

And like a dying lady, lean and pale,
Who totters forth, wrapped in a gauzy veil,
Out of her chamber, led by the insane
And feeble wanderings of her fading brain,
The moon arose up in the murky East,
A white and shapeless mass—

TO NIGHT

Swiftly walk o'er the western wave,
    Spirit of Night!
Out of the misty eastern cave
Where, all the long and lone daylight
Thou wovest dreams of joy and fear,
Which make thee terrible and dear,
    Swift be thy flight!

Wrap thy form in a mantle gray,
    Star-inwrought!
Blind with thine hair the eyes of day,
Kiss her until she be wearied out—
Then wander o'er City and sea and land,
Touching all with thine opiate wand—
    Come, long-sought!

When I arose and saw the dawn
    I sighed for thee;
When Light rode high, and the dew was gone,
And noon lay heavy on flower and tree,
And the weary Day turned to his rest,
Lingering like an unloved guest,
    I sighed for thee.

Thy brother Death came, and cried,
    Wouldst thou me?
Thy sweet child Sleep, the filmy-eyed,
Murmured like a noontide bee,
Shall I nestle near thy side?
Wouldst thou me? and I replied,
    No, not thee!

Death will come when thou art dead,
　　Soon, too soon—
Sleep will come when thou art fled;
Of neither would I ask the boon
I ask of thee, beloved Night—
Swift be thine approaching flight,
　　Come soon, soon!

TIME

Unfathomable Sea! whose waves are years,
　Ocean of Time, whose waters of deep woe
Are brackish with the salt of human tears!
　Thou shoreless flood, which in thy ebb and flow
Claspest the limits of mortality,
　And sick of prey, yet howling on for more,
Vomitest thy wrecks on its inhospitable shore;
　Treacherous in calm, and terrible in storm,
　　Who shall put forth on thee,
　　Unfathomable Sea!

TO ——

Music when soft voices die,
Vibrates in the memory—
Odors, when sweet violets sicken,
Live within the sense they quicken.

Rose leaves, when the rose is dead,
Are heaped for the belovèd's bed;
And so thy thoughts, when thou art gone,
Love itself shall slumber on.

A LAMENT

O World, O Life, O Time,
On whose last steps I climb,
Trembling at that where I had stood before,
When will return the glory of your prime?
No more, O nevermore!

Out of the day and night
A joy has taken flight—
Fresh spring and summer [   ] and winter hoar
Move my faint heart with grief, but with delight
No more, O nevermore!

CHORUSES FROM *HELLAS*

I

Worlds on worlds are rolling ever
　From creation to decay,
Like the bubbles on a river
　Sparkling, bursting, borne away.
　But they are still immortal
　Who, through birth's orient portal
And death's dark chasm hurrying to and fro,
　Clothe their unceasing flight
　In the brief dust and light
Gathered around their chariots as they go;
　New shapes they still may weave,
　New gods, new laws receive,
Bright or dim are they as the robes they last
　On Death's bare ribs had cast.

A power from the unknown God,
　A Promethean conqueror, came;
Like a triumphal path he trod
　The thorns of death and shame.
　A mortal shape to him
　Was like the vapor dim
Which the orient planet animates with light;
　Hell, Sin, and Slavery came,
　Like bloodhounds mild and tame,
Nor preyed, until their Lord had taken flight;
　The moon of Mahomet
　Arose, and it shall set:
While blazoned as on Heaven's immortal noon
　The cross leads generations on.

Swift as the radiant shapes of sleep
   From one whose dreams are Paradise
Fly, when the fond wretch wakes to weep,
   And Day peers forth with her blank eyes;
   So fleet, so faint, so fair,
   The Powers of earth and air
Fled from the folding-star of Bethlehem:
   Apollo, Pan, and Love,
   And even Olympian Jove
Grew weak, for killing Truth had glared on them;
   Our hills and seas and streams,
   Dispeopled of their dreams,
Their waters turned to blood, their dew to tears,
   Wailed for the golden years.

II

The world's great age begins anew,
   The golden years return,
The earth doth like a snake renew
   Her winter weeds outworn:
Heaven smiles, and faiths and empires gleam,
Like wrecks of a dissolving dream.

A brighter Hellas rears its mountains
   From waves serener far;
A new Peneus rolls his fountains
   Against the morning star.
Where fairer Tempes bloom, there sleep
Young Cyclads on a sunnier deep.

A loftier Argo cleaves the main,
   Fraught with a later prize;
Another Orpheus sings again,
   And loves, and weeps, and dies.
A new Ulysses leaves once more
Calypso for his native shore.

Oh, write no more the tale of Troy,
    If earth Death's scroll must be!
Nor mix with Laian rage the joy
    Which dawns upon the free:
Although a subtler Sphinx renew
Riddles of death Thebes never knew.

Another Athens shall arise,
    And to remoter time
Bequeath, like sunset to the skies,
    The splendor of its prime;
And leave, if naught so bright may live,
All earth can take or Heaven can give.

Saturn and Love their long repose
    Shall burst, more bright and good
Than all who fell, than One who rose,
    Than many unsubdued:
Not gold, not blood, their altar dowers,
But votive tears and symbol flowers.

Oh, cease! must hate and death return?
    Cease! must men kill and die?
Cease! drain not to its dregs the urn
    Of bitter prophecy.
The world is weary of the past,
Oh, might it die or rest at last!

TO EMILIA VIVIANI

I

Madonna, wherefore hast thou sent to me
   Sweet-basil and mignonette?
Embleming love and health, which never yet
In the same wreath might be.
   Alas, and they are wet!
Is it with thy kisses or thy tears?
     For never rain or dew
     Such fragrance drew
From plant or flower—the very doubt endears
   My sadness ever new,
The sighs I breathe, the tears I shed for thee.

II

Send the stars light, but send not love to me,
   In whom love ever made
Health like a heap of embers soon to fade—

SONG

Rarely, rarely comest thou,
   Spirit of Delight!
Wherefore hast thou left me now
   Many a day and night?
Many a weary night and day
'Tis since thou art fled away.

How shall ever one like me
   Win thee back again?
With the joyous and the free
   Thou wilt scoff at pain.
Spirit false! thou hast forgot
All but those who need thee not.

As a lizard with the shade
   Of a trembling leaf,
Thou with sorrow art dismayed;
   Even the sighs of grief
Reproach thee, that thou art not near,
And reproach thou wilt not hear.

Let me set my mournful ditty
   To a merry measure;
Thou wilt never come for pity—
   Thou wilt come for pleasure;
Pity then will cut away
Those cruel wings, and thou wilt stay—

I love all that thou lovest,
   Spirit of Delight!
The fresh Earth in new leaves dressed,

And the starry night,
Autumn evening, and the morn
When the golden mists are born.

I love snow, and all the forms
   Of the radiant frost;
I love waves and winds and storms—
   Every thing almost
Which is Nature's and may be
Untainted by man's misery.

I love tranquil Solitude,
   And such society
As is quiet, wise and good;
   Between thee and me
What difference? but thou dost possess
The things I seek—not love them less.

I love Love—though he has wings,
   And like light can flee—
But above all other things,
   Spirit, I love thee—
Thou art Love and Life! O come,
Make once more my heart thy home.

WRITTEN ON HEARING THE NEWS OF
THE DEATH OF NAPOLEON

I

What! alive and so bold, oh Earth?
  Art thou not overbold?
  What! leapest thou forth as of old
In the light of thy morning mirth,
The last of the flock of the starry fold?
Ha! leapest thou forth as of old?
Are not the limbs still when the ghost is fled,
And canst thou move, Napoleon being dead?

II

How! is not thy quick heart cold?
  What spark is alive on thy hearth?
How! is not *his* death-knell knolled?
  And livest *thou* still, Mother Earth?
Thou wert warming thy fingers old
O'er the embers covered and cold
Of that most fiery spirit, when it fled—
What, Mother, do you laugh now he is dead?

III

"Who has known me of old," replied Earth,
  "Or who has my story told?
  It is thou who art overbold."
  And the lightning of scorn laughed forth
  As she sung, "To my bosom I fold
All my sons when their knell is knolled
And so with living motion all are fed
And the quick spring like weeds out of the dead.

IV

"Still alive and still bold," shouted Earth,
  "I grow bolder and still more bold.
   The dead fill me ten thousand fold
Fuller of speed and splendor and mirth.
I was cloudy, and sullen, and cold,
Like a frozen chaos uprolled
Till by the spirit of the mighty dead
My heart grew warm. I feed on whom I fed.

V

"Aye, alive and still bold," muttered Earth,
  "Napoleon's fierce spirit rolled,
   In terror, and blood, and gold,
A torrent of ruin to death from his birth.
Leave the millions who follow to mold
The metal before it be cold,
And weave into his shame, which like the dead
Shrouds me, the hopes that from his glory fled."

REMEMBRANCE

I

Swifter far than summer's flight—
Swifter far than youth's delight—
Swifter far than happy night,
   Art thou come and gone—
As the earth when leaves are dead,
As the night when sleep is sped,
As the heart when joy is fled,
   I am left lone, alone.

II

The swallow summer comes again—
The owlet night resumes her reign—
But the wild-swan youth is fain
   To fly with thee, false as thou—
My heart each day desires the morrow;
Sleep itself is turned to sorrow;
Vainly would my winter borrow
   Sunny leaves from any bough.

III

Lilies for a bridal bed—
Roses for a matron's head—
Violets for a maiden dead—
   Pansies let *my* flowers be:
On the living grave I bear
Scatter them without a tear—
Let no friend, however dear,
   Waste one hope, one fear for me.

TO EDWARD WILLIAMS

I

The serpent is shut out from Paradise.
  The wounded deer must seek the herb no more
    In which its heart-cure lies:
  The widowed dove must cease to haunt a bower
Like that from which its mate with feignèd sighs
    Fled in the April hour.
  I too must seldom seek again
Near happy friends a mitigated pain.

II

Of hatred I am proud—with scorn content;
  Indifference, that once hurt me, now is grown
    Itself indifferent;
  But, not to speak of love, pity alone
Can break a spirit already more than bent.
    The miserable one
  Turns the mind's poison into food—
Its medicine is tears—its evil good.

III

Therefore, if now I see you seldomer,
  Dear friends, dear *friend!* know that I only fly
    Your looks, because they stir
  Griefs that should sleep, and hopes that cannot die:
The very comfort that they minister
    I scarce can bear, yet I,
  So deeply is the arrow gone,
Should quickly perish if it were withdrawn.

IV

When I return to my cold home, you ask
   Why I am not as I have ever been.
     You spoil me for the task
   Of acting a forced part in life's dull scene—
Of wearing on my brow the idle mask
     Of author, great or mean,
   In the world's carnival. I sought
Peace thus, and but in you I found it not.

V

Full half an hour, today, I tried my lot
   With various flowers, and every one still said,
     "She loves me—loves me not."
   And if this meant a vision long since fled—
If it meant fortune, fame, or peace of thought—
     If it meant—but I dread
   To speak what you may know too well:
Still there was truth in the sad oracle.

VI

The crane o'er seas and forests seeks her home;
   No bird so wild but has its quiet nest,
     When it no more would roam;
   The sleepless billows on the ocean's breast
Break like a bursting heart, and die in foam,
     And thus at length find rest:
   Doubtless there is a place of peace
Where *my* weak heart and all its throbs will cease.

VII

I asked her, yesterday, if she believed
   That I had resolution. One who *had*
     Would ne'er have thus relieved

His heart with words—but what his judgement bade
Would do, and leave the scorner unrelieved.
　　These verses are too sad
　To send to you, but that I know,
Happy yourself, you feel another's woe.

TO ——

I

One word is too often profaned
　For me to profane it,
One feeling too falsely disdained
　For thee to disdain it;
One hope is too like despair
　For prudence to smother,
And pity from thee more dear
　Than that from another.

II

I can give not what men call love,
　But wilt thou accept not
The worship the heart lifts above
　And the Heavens reject not—
The desire of the moth for the star,
　Of the night for the morrow,
The devotion to something afar
　From the sphere of our sorrow?

TO ——

I

When passion's trance is overpast,
If tenderness and truth could last,
Or live, whilst all wild feelings keep
Some mortal slumber, dark and deep,
I should not weep, I should not weep!

II

It were enough to feel, to see,
Thy soft eyes gazing tenderly,
And dream the rest—and burn and be
The secret food of fires unseen,
Couldst thou but be as thou hast been.

III

After the slumber of the year
The woodland violets reappear;
All things revive in field or grove,
And sky and sea, but two, which move
And form all others, life and love.

MUTABILITY

The flower that smiles today
    Tomorrow dies;
All that we wish to stay
    Tempts and then flies;
What is this world's delight?
Lightning, that mocks the night,
    Brief even as bright—

Virtue, how frail it is!—
    Friendship, how rare!—
Love, how it sells poor bliss
    For proud despair!
But these though soon they fall,
Survive their joy, and all
    Which ours we call—

Whilst skies are blue and bright,
    Whilst flowers are gay,
Whilst eyes that change ere night
    Make glad the day;
Whilst yet the calm hours creep,
Dream thou—and from thy sleep
    Then wake to weep.

WHEN THE LAMP IS SHATTERED

When the lamp is shattered
The light in the dust lies dead—
When the cloud is scattered
The rainbow's glory is shed—
When the lute is broken
Sweet tones are remembered not—
When the lips have spoken
Loved accents are soon forgot.

As music and splendor
Survive not the lamp and the lute,
The heart's echoes render
No song when the spirit is mute—
No song—but sad dirges
Like the wind through a ruined cell
Or the mournful surges
That ring the dead seaman's knell.

When hearts have once mingled
Love first leaves the well-built nest—
The weak one is singled
To endure what it once possessed.
O Love! who bewailest
The frailty of all things here,
Why choose you the frailest
For your cradle, your home and your bier?

Its passions will rock thee
As the storms rock the ravens on high—
Bright Reason will mock thee
Like the Sun from a wintry sky—

From thy nest every rafter
Will rot, and thine eagle home
Leave thee naked to laughter
When leaves fall and cold winds come.

A DIRGE

Rough wind, that moanest loud
Grief too sad for song;
Wild wind, when sullen cloud
Knells all the night long;
Sad storm, whose tears are vain,
Bare woods, whose branches strain,
Deep caves and dreary main—
Wail, for the world's wrong!

TO JANE. THE INVITATION

Best and brightest, come away—
Fairer far than this fair day
Which like thee to those in sorrow
Comes to bid a sweet good-morrow
To the rough year just awake
In its cradle on the brake—
The brightest hour of unborn spring
Through the winter wandering
Found, it seems, this halcyon morn
To hoar February born;
Bending from Heaven in azure mirth
It kissed the forehead of the earth
And smiled upon the silent sea,
And bade the frozen streams be free
And waked to music all their fountains,
And breathed upon the frozen mountains,
And like a prophetess of May
Strewed flowers upon the barren way,
Making the wintry world appear
Like one on whom thou smilest, dear.

Away, away from men and towns
To the wild wood and the downs,
To the silent wilderness
Where the soul need not repress
Its music lest it should not find
An echo in another's mind,
While the touch of Nature's art
Harmonizes heart to heart—
I leave this notice on my door
For each accustomed visitor—
"I am gone into the fields
To take what this sweet hour yields.
Reflection, you may come tomorrow,
Sit by the fireside with Sorrow—

You, with the unpaid bill, Despair,
You, tiresome verse-reciter Care,
I will pay you in the grave,
Death will listen to your stave—
Expectation too, be off!
Today is for itself enough—
Hope, in pity mock not woe
With smiles, nor follow where I go;
Long having lived on thy sweet food,
At length I find one moment's good
After long pain—with all your love
This you never told me of."

Radiant Sister of the day,
Awake, arise and come away
To the wild woods and the plains
And the pools where winter rains
Image all their roof of leaves,
Where the pine its garland weaves
Of sapless green and ivy dun
Round stems that never kiss the Sun—
Where the lawns and pastures be
And the sandhills of the sea—
Where the melting hoarfrost wets
The daisy-star that never sets,
And windflowers, and violets
Which yet join not scent to hue
Crown the pale year weak and new,
When the night is left behind
In the deep east dun and blind
And the blue noon is over us,
And the multitudinous
Billows murmur at our feet
Where the earth and ocean meet,
And all things seem only one
In the universal Sun—

TO JANE. THE RECOLLECTION

February 2, 1822

Now the last day of many days,
All beautiful and bright as thou,
The loveliest and the last, is dead.
Rise, Memory, and write its praise!
Up to thy wonted work! come, trace
The epitaph of glory fled;
For now the Earth has changed its face,
A frown is on the Heaven's brow.

I

We wandered to the pine forest
   That skirts the ocean foam;
The lightest wind was in its nest,
   The Tempest in its home;
The whispering waves were half asleep,
   The clouds were gone to play,
And on the bosom of the deep
   The smile of Heaven lay;
It seemed as if the hour were one
   Sent from beyond the skies,
Which scattered from above the sun
   A light of Paradise.

II

We paused amid the pines that stood
   The giants of the waste,
Tortured by storms to shapes as rude
   As serpents interlaced,
And soothed by every azure breath

That under Heaven is blown
To harmonies and hues beneath,
   As tender as its own;
Now all the treetops lay asleep
   Like green waves on the sea,
As still as in the silent deep
   The Ocean woods may be.

III

How calm it was! the silence there
   By such a chain was bound
That even the busy woodpecker
   Made stiller with her sound
The inviolable quietness;
   The breath of peace we drew
With its soft motion made not less
   The calm that round us grew—
There seemed from the remotest seat
   Of the white mountain waste,
To the soft flower beneath our feet
   A magic circle traced,
A spirit interfused around
   A thrilling silent life,
To momentary peace it bound
   Our mortal nature's strife—
And still I felt the center of
   The magic circle there
Was one fair form that filled with love
   The lifeless atmosphere.

IV

We paused beside the pools that lie
   Under the forest bough—
Each seemed as 'twere, a little sky
   Gulfed in a world below;

A firmament of purple light
   Which in the dark earth lay
More boundless than the depth of night
   And purer than the day,
In which the lovely forests grew
   As in the upper air,
More perfect, both in shape and hue,
   Than any spreading there;
There lay the glade, the neighboring lawn,
   And through the dark green wood
The white sun twinkling like the dawn
   Out of a speckled cloud.

v

Sweet views, which in our world above
   Can never well be seen,
Were imaged in the water's love
   Of that fair forest green;
And all was interfused beneath
   With an Elysian glow,
An atmosphere without a breath,
   A softer day below—
Like one beloved, the scene had lent
   To the dark water's breast,
Its every leaf and lineament
   With more than truth expressed;
Until an envious wind crept by,
   Like an unwelcome thought
Which from the mind's too faithful eye
   Blots one dear image out—
Though thou art ever fair and kind
   And forests ever green,
Less oft is peace in S[helley]'s mind
   Than calm in water seen.

WITH A GUITAR.
TO JANE

Ariel to Miranda—Take
This slave of music for the sake
Of him who is the slave of thee;
And teach it all the harmony,
In which thou can'st, and only thou,
Make the delighted spirit glow,
Till joy denies itself again
And too intense is turned to pain;
For by permission and command
Of thine own prince Ferdinand
Poor Ariel sends this silent token
Of more than ever can be spoken;
Your guardian spirit Ariel, who
From life to life must still pursue
Your happiness, for thus alone
Can Ariel ever find his own;
From Prospero's enchanted cell,
As the mighty verses tell,
To the throne of Naples he
Lit you o'er the trackless sea,
Flitting on, your prow before,
Like a living meteor.
When you die, the silent Moon
In her interlunar swoon
Is not sadder in her cell
Than deserted Ariel;
When you live again on Earth
Like an unseen Star of birth
Ariel guides you o'er the sea
Of life from your nativity;

Many changes have been run
Since Ferdinand and you begun
Your course of love, and Ariel still
Has tracked your steps and served your will;
Now, in humbler, happier lot
This is all remembered not;
And now, alas! the poor sprite is
Imprisoned for some fault of his
In a body like a grave—
From you, he only dares to crave
For his service and his sorrow
A smile today, a song tomorrow.

The artist who this idol wrought
To echo all harmonious thought
Felled a tree, while on the steep
The woods were in their winter sleep
Rocked in that repose divine
On the windswept Apennine;
And dreaming, some of autumn past
And some of spring approaching fast,
And some of April buds and showers
And some of songs in July bowers
And all of love—and so this tree—
O that such our death may be—
Died in sleep, and felt no pain,
To live in happier form again,
From which, beneath Heaven's fairest star,
The artist wrought this loved guitar,
And taught it justly to reply
To all who question skillfully
In language gentle as thine own;
Whispering in enamored tone
Sweet oracles of woods and dells
And summer winds in sylvan cells
For it had learnt all harmonies

Of the plains and of the skies,
Of the forests and the mountains,
And the many-voiced fountains,
The clearest echoes of the hills,
The softest notes of falling rills,
The melodies of birds and bees,
The murmuring of summer seas,
And pattering rain and breathing dew
And airs of evening—and it knew
That seldom heard mysterious sound,
Which, driven on its diurnal round
As it floats through boundless day
Our world enkindles on its way—
All this it knows, but will not tell
To those who cannot question well
The spirit that inhabits it:
It talks according to the wit
Of its companions, and no more
Is heard than has been felt before
By those who tempt it to betray
These secrets of an elder day—
But, sweetly as its answers will
Flatter hands of perfect skill,
It keeps its highest holiest tone
For our beloved Jane alone.

TO JANE

The keen stars were twinkling
And the fair moon was rising among them,
 Dear Jane.
The guitar was tinkling
But the notes were not sweet till you sung them
 Again—
As the moon's soft splendor
O'er the faint cold starlight of Heaven
 Is thrown—
So your voice most tender
To the strings without soul had then given
 Its own.

The stars will awaken,
Though the moon sleep a full hour later,
 Tonight;
No leaf will be shaken
While the dews of your melody scatter
 Delight.
Though the sound overpowers
Sing again, with your dear voice revealing
 A tone
Of some world far from ours,
Where music and moonlight and feeling
 Are one.

LINES WRITTEN IN THE BAY OF LERICI

Bright wanderer, fair coquette of Heaven,
To whom alone it has been given
To change and be adored forever. . . .
Envy not this dim world, for never
But once within its shadow grew
One fair as [thou], but far more true.
She left me at the silent time
When the moon had ceased to climb
The azure dome of Heaven's steep,
And like an albatross asleep,
Balanced on her wings of light,
Hovered in the purple night,
Ere she sought her Ocean nest
In the chambers of the west—
She left me, and I stayed alone
Thinking over every tone,
Which though now silent to the ear
The enchanted heart could hear
Like notes which die when born, but still
Haunt the echoes of the hill:
And feeling ever—O too much—
The soft vibrations of her touch
As if her gentle hand even now
Lightly trembled on my brow;
And thus although she absent were
Memory gave me all of her
That even fancy dares to claim—
Her presence had made weak and tame
All passions, and I lived alone,
In the time which is our own;
The past and future were forgot

As they had been, and would be, not—
But soon, the guardian angel gone,
The demon reassumed his throne
In my faint heart . . . I dare not speak
My thoughts; but thus disturbed and weak
I sate and watched the vessels glide
Along the ocean bright and wide,
Like spirit-winged chariots sent
O'er some serenest element
To ministrations strange and far;
As if to some Elysian star
They sailed for drink to medicine
Such sweet and bitter pain as mine.
And the wind that winged their flight
From the land came fresh and light,
And the scent of sleeping flowers
And the coolness of the hours
Of dew, and the sweet warmth of day
Was scattered o'er the twinkling bay;
And the fisher with his lamp
And spear, about the low rocks damp
Crept, and struck the fish who came
To worship the delusive flame:
Too happy, they whose pleasure sought
Extinguishes all sense and thought
Of the regret that pleasure [   ]
Destroying life alone not peace.

Alastor

OR, THE SPIRIT OF
SOLITUDE

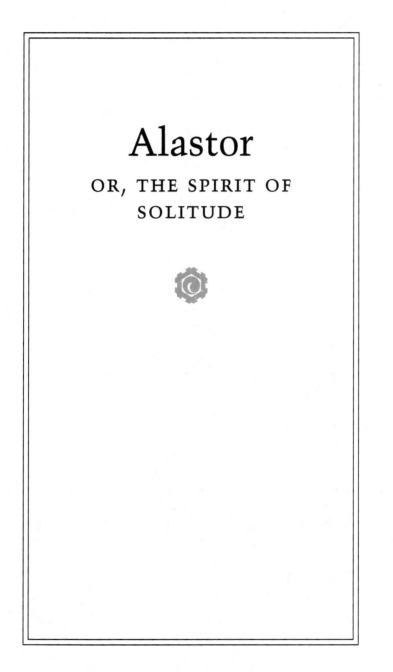

ALASTOR;
OR, THE SPIRIT OF SOLITUDE

Preface

The poem entitled "Alastor," may be considered as
allegorical of one of the most interesting situations of
the human mind. It represents a youth of uncorrupted
feelings and adventurous genius led forth by an imagination inflamed and purified through familiarity with
all that is excellent and majestic, to the contemplation
of the universe. He drinks deep of the fountains of
knowledge, and is still insatiate. The magnificence and
beauty of the external world sinks profoundly into the
frame of his conceptions, and affords to their
modifications a variety not to be exhausted. So long as
it is possible for his desires to point towards objects
thus infinite and unmeasured, he is joyous, and tranquil, and self-possessed. But the period arrives when
these objects cease to suffice. His mind is at length
suddenly awakened and thirsts for intercourse with an
intelligence similar to itself. He images to himself the
Being whom he loves. Conversant with speculations of
the sublimest and most perfect natures, the vision in
which he embodies his own imaginations unites all of
wonderful, or wise, or beautiful, which the poet, the
philosopher, or the lover could depicture. The intel-
lectual faculties, the imagination, the functions of
sense, have their respective requisitions on the sympathy of corresponding powers in other human beings.
The Poet is represented as uniting these requisitions,
and attaching them to a single image. He seeks in vain
for a prototype of his conception. Blasted by his disappointment, he descends to an untimely grave.

The picture is not barren of instruction to actual men. The Poet's self-centered seclusion was avenged by the furies of an irresistible passion pursuing him to speedy ruin. But that Power which strikes the luminaries of the world with sudden darkness and extinction, by awakening them to too exquisite a perception of its influences, dooms to a slow and poisonous decay those meaner spirits that dare to abjure its dominion. Their destiny is more abject and inglorious as their delinquency is more contemptible and pernicious. They who, deluded by no generous error, instigated by no sacred thirst of doubtful knowledge, duped by no illustrious superstition, loving nothing on this earth, and cherishing no hopes beyond, yet keep aloof from sympathies with their kind, rejoicing neither in human joy nor mourning with human grief; these, and such as they, have their apportioned curse. They languish, because none feel with them their common nature. They are morally dead. They are neither friends, nor lovers, nor fathers, nor citizens of the world, nor benefactors of their country. Among those who attempt to exist without human sympathy, the pure and tenderhearted perish through the intensity and passion of their search after its communities, when the vacancy of their spirit suddenly makes itself felt. All else, selfish, blind, and torpid, are those unforeseeing multitudes who constitute, together with their own, the lasting misery and loneliness of the world. Those who love not their fellow-beings live unfruitful lives, and prepare for their old age a miserable grave.

> "The good die first,
> And those whose hearts are dry as summer dust,
> Burn to the socket!"

December 14, 1815.

ALASTOR;
OR, THE SPIRIT OF SOLITUDE

Nondum amabam, et amare amabam, quaerebam
quid amarem, amans amare—
Confessions, St. Augustine

Earth, ocean, air, beloved brotherhood!
If our great Mother has imbued my soul
With aught of natural piety to feel
Your love, and recompense the boon with mine;
If dewy morn, and odorous noon, and even,
With sunset and its gorgeous ministers,
And solemn midnight's tingling silentness;
If autumn's hollow sighs in the sere wood,
And winter robing with pure snow and crowns
Of starry ice the gray grass and bare boughs;
If spring's voluptuous pantings when she breathes
Her first sweet kisses, have been dear to me;
If no bright bird, insect, or gentle beast
I consciously have injured, but still loved
And cherished these my kindred; then forgive
This boast, beloved brethren, and withdraw
No portion of your wonted favor now!

Mother of this unfathomable world!
Favor my solemn song, for I have loved
Thee ever, and thee only; I have watched
Thy shadow, and the darkness of thy steps,
And my heart ever gazes on the depth
Of thy deep mysteries. I have made my bed
In charnels and on coffins, where black death
Keeps record of the trophies won from thee.
Hoping to still these obstinate questionings
Of thee and thine, by forcing some lone ghost,
Thy messenger, to render up the tale

Of what we are. In lone and silent hours,
When night makes a weird sound of its own stillness,
Like an inspired and desperate alchemist
Staking his very life on some dark hope,
Have I mixed awful talk and asking looks
With my most innocent love, until strange tears
Uniting with those breathless kisses, made
Such magic as compels the charmed night
To render up thy charge: . . . and, though ne'er yet
Thou hast unveil'd thy inmost sanctuary,
Enough from incommunicable dream,
And twilight phantasms, and deep noonday thought,
Has shone within me, that serenely now
And moveless, as a long-forgotten lyre
Suspended in the solitary dome
Of some mysterious and deserted fane,
I wait thy breath, Great Parent, that my strain
May modulate with murmurs of the air,
And motions of the forests and the sea,
And voice of living beings, and woven hymns
Of night and day, and the deep heart of man.

    There was a Poet whose untimely tomb
No human hands with pious reverence reared,
But the charmed eddies of autumnal winds
Built o'er his moldering bones a pyramid
Of moldering leaves in the waste wilderness—
A lovely youth—no mourning maiden decked
With weeping flowers, or votive cypress wreath,
The lone couch of his everlasting sleep—
Gentle, and brave, and generous—no lorn bard
Breathed o'er his dark fate one melodious sigh:
He lived, he died, he sung, in solitude.
Strangers have wept to hear his passionate notes,
And virgins, as unknown he past, have pined
And wasted for fond love of his wild eyes.

The fire of those soft orbs has ceased to burn,
And Silence, too enamored of that voice,
Locks its mute music in her rugged cell.

By solemn vision, and bright silver dream,
His infancy was nurtured. Every sight
And sound from the vast earth and ambient air,
Sent to his heart its choicest impulses.
The fountains of divine philosophy
Fled not his thirsting lips, and all of great
Or good, or lovely, which the sacred past
In truth or fable consecrates, he felt
And knew. When early youth had past, he left
His cold fireside and alienated home
To seek strange truths in undiscovered lands.
Many a wide waste and tangled wilderness
Has lured his fearless steps; and he has bought
With his sweet voice and eyes, from savage men,
His rest and food. Nature's most secret steps
He like her shadow has pursued, where'er
The red volcano overcanopies
Its fields of snow and pinnacles of ice
With burning smoke, or where bitumen lakes
On black bare pointed islets ever beat
With sluggish surge, or where the secret caves
Rugged and dark, winding among the springs
Of fire and poison, inaccessible
To avarice or pride, their starry domes
Of diamond and of gold expand above
Numberless and immeasurable halls,
Frequent with crystal column, and clear shrines
Of pearl, and thrones radiant with chrysolite.
Nor had that scene of ampler majesty
Than gems or gold, the varying roof of heaven
And the green earth lost in his heart its claims
To love and wonder; he would linger long

In lonesome vales, making the wild his home,
Until the doves and squirrels would partake
From his innocuous hand his bloodless food,
Lured by the gentle meaning of his looks,
And the wild antelope, that starts whene'er
The dry leaf rustles in the brake, suspend
Her timid steps to gaze upon a form
More graceful than her own.

                   His wandering step
Obedient to high thoughts, has visited
The awful ruins of the days of old:
Athens, and Tyre, and Balbec, and the waste
Where stood Jerusalem, the fallen towers
Of Babylon, the eternal pyramids,
Memphis and Thebes, and whatsoe'er of strange
Sculptured on alabaster obelisk,
Or jasper tomb, or mutilated sphinx,
Dark Ethiopia in her desert hills
Conceals. Among the ruined temples there,
Stupendous columns, and wild images
Of more than man, where marble daemons watch
The Zodiac's brazen mystery, and dead men
Hang their mute thoughts on the mute walls around,
He lingered, poring on memorials
Of the world's youth, through the long burning day
Gazed on those speechless shapes, nor, when the moon
Filled the mysterious halls with floating shades
Suspended he that task, but ever gazed
And gazed, till meaning on his vacant mind
Flashed like strong inspiration, and he saw
The thrilling secrets of the birth of time.

Meanwhile an Arab maiden brought his food,
Her daily portion, from her father's tent,
And spread her matting for his couch, and stole

From duties and repose to tend his steps—
Enamored, yet not daring for deep awe
To speak her love—and watched his nightly sleep,
Sleepless herself, to gaze upon his lips
Parted in slumber, whence the regular breath
Of innocent dreams arose: then, when red morn
Made paler the pale moon, to her cold home
Wildered, and wan, and panting, she returned.

The Poet wandering on, through Arabie
And Persia, and the wild Carmanian waste,
And o'er the aerial mountains which pour down
Indus and Oxus from their icy caves,
In joy and exultation held his way;
Till in the vale of Kashmir, far within
Its loneliest dell, where odorous plants entwine
Beneath the hollow rocks a natural bower,
Beside a sparkling rivulet he stretched
His languid limbs. A vision on his sleep
There came, a dream of hopes that never yet
Had flushed his cheek. He dreamed a veiled maid
Sate near him, talking in low solemn tones.
Her voice was like the voice of his own soul
Heard in the calm of thought; its music long,
Like woven sounds of streams and breezes, held
His inmost sense suspended in its web
Of many-colored woof and shifting hues.
Knowledge and truth and virtue were her theme,
And lofty hopes of divine liberty,
Thoughts the most dear to him, and poesy,
Herself a poet. Soon the solemn mood
Of her pure mind kindled through all her frame
A permeating fire: wild numbers then
She raised, with voice stifled in tremulous sobs
Subdued by its own pathos: her fair hands
Were bare alone, sweeping from some strange harp

Strange symphony, and in their branching veins
The eloquent blood told an ineffable tale.
The beating of her heart was heard to fill
The pauses of her music, and her breath
Tumultuously accorded with those fits
Of intermitted song. Sudden she rose,
As if her heart impatiently endured
Its bursting burthen: at the sound he turned,
And saw by the warm light of their own life
Her glowing limbs beneath the sinuous veil
Of woven wind, her outspread arms now bare,
Her dark locks floating in the breath of night,
Her beamy bending eyes, her parted lips
Outstretched, and pale, and quivering eagerly.
His strong heart sunk and sickened with excess
Of love. He reared his shuddering limbs and quelled
His gasping breath, and spread his arms to meet
Her panting bosom: . . . she drew back a while,
Then, yielding to the irresistible joy,
With frantic gesture and short breathless cry
Folded his frame in her dissolving arms.
Now blackness veiled his dizzy eyes, and night
Involved and swallowed up the vision; sleep,
Like a dark flood suspended in its course,
Rolled back its impulse on his vacant brain.

Roused by the shock he started from his trance—
The cold white light of morning, the blue moon
Low in the west, the clear and garish hills,
The distinct valley and the vacant woods,
Spread round him where he stood. Whither have fled
The hues of heaven that canopied his bower
Of yesternight? The sounds that soothed his sleep,
The mystery and the majesty of Earth,
The joy, the exultation? His wan eyes
Gaze on the empty scene as vacantly

As ocean's moon looks on the moon in heaven.
The spirit of sweet human love has sent
A vision to the sleep of him who spurned
Her choicest gifts. He eagerly pursues
Beyond the realms of dream that fleeting shade;
He overleaps the bounds. Alas! alas!
Were limbs, and breath, and being intertwined
Thus treacherously? Lost, lost, forever lost,
In the wide pathless desert of dim sleep,
That beautiful shape! Does the dark gate of death
Conduct to thy mysterious paradise,
O Sleep? Does the bright arch of rainbow clouds,
And pendent mountains seen in the calm lake,
Lead only to a black and watery depth,
While death's blue vault, with loathliest vapors hung,
Where every shade which the foul grave exhales
Hides its dead eye from the detested day,
Conduct, O Sleep, to thy delightful realms?
This doubt with sudden tide flowed on his heart,
The insatiate hope which it awakened, stung
His brain even like despair.
                                    While daylight held
The sky, the Poet kept mute conference
With his still soul. At night the passion came,
Like the fierce fiend of a distempered dream,
And shook him from his rest, and led him forth
Into the darkness—As an eagle grasped
In folds of the green serpent, feels her breast
Burn with the poison, and precipitates
Through night and day, tempest, and calm, and cloud,
Frantic with dizzying anguish, her blind flight
O'er the wide aery wilderness: thus driven
By the bright shadow of that lovely dream,
Beneath the cold glare of the desolate night,
Through tangled swamps and deep precipitous dells,
Startling with careless step the moonlight snake,

He fled. Red morning dawned upon his flight,
Shedding the mockery of its vital hues
Upon his cheek of death. He wandered on
Till vast Aornos seen from Petra's steep
Hung o'er the low horizon like a cloud;
Through Balk, and where the desolated tombs
Of Parthian kings scatter to every wind
Their wasting dust, wildly he wandered on,
Day after day, a weary waste of hours,
Bearing within his life the brooding care
That ever fed on its decaying flame.
And now his limbs were lean; his scattered hair
Sered by the autumn of strange suffering
Sung dirges in the wind; his listless hand
Hung like dead bone within its withered skin;
Life, and the luster that consumed it, shone
As in a furnace burning secretly
From his dark eyes alone. The cottagers,
Who ministered with human charity
His human wants, beheld with wondering awe
Their fleeting visitant. The mountaineer,
Encountering on some dizzy precipice
That spectral form, deemed that the Spirit of wind
With lightning eyes, and eager breath, and feet
Disturbing not the drifted snow, had paused
In its career: the infant would conceal
His troubled visage in his mother's robe
In terror at the glare of those wild eyes,
To remember their strange light in many a dream
Of aftertimes; but youthful maidens, taught
By nature, would interpret half the woe
That wasted him, would call him with false names
Brother, and friend, would press his pallid hand
At parting, and watch, dim through tears, the path
Of his departure from their father's door.

At length upon the lone Chorasmian shore
He paused, a wide and melancholy waste
Of putrid marshes. A strong impulse urged
His steps to the seashore. A swan was there,
Beside a sluggish stream among the reeds.
It rose as he approached, and with strong wings
Scaling the upward sky, bent its bright course
High over the immeasurable main.
His eyes pursued its flight—"Thou hast a home,
Beautiful bird; thou voyagest to thine home,
Where thy sweet mate will twine her downy neck
With thine, and welcome thy return with eyes
Bright in the luster of their own fond joy.
And what am I that I should linger here;
With voice far sweeter than thy dying notes,
Spirit more vast than thine, frame more attuned
To beauty, wasting these surpassing powers
In the deaf air, to the blind earth, and heaven
That echoes not my thoughts?" A gloomy smile
Of desperate hope wrinkled his quivering lips.
For sleep, he knew, kept most relentlessly
Its precious charge, and silent death exposed,
Faithless perhaps as sleep, a shadowy lure,
With doubtful smile mocking its own strange charms.

Startled by his own thoughts he looked around.
There was no fair fiend near him, not a sight
Or sound of awe but in his own deep mind.
A little shallop floating near the shore
Caught the impatient wandering of his gaze.
It had been long abandoned, for its sides
Gaped wide with many a rift, and its frail joints
Swayed with the undulations of the tide.
A restless impulse urged him to embark
And meet lone Death on the drear ocean's waste;
For well he knew that mighty Shadow loves
The slimy caverns of the populous deep.

The day was fair and sunny; sea and sky
Drank its inspiring radiance, and the wind
Swept strongly from the shore, blackening the waves.
Following his eager soul, the wanderer
Leaped in the boat, he spread his cloak aloft
On the bare mast, and took his lonely seat,
And felt the boat speed o'er the tranquil sea
Like a torn cloud before the hurricane.

As one that in a silver vision floats
Obedient to the sweep of odorous winds
Upon resplendent clouds, so rapidly
Along the dark and ruffled waters fled
The straining boat—A whirlwind swept it on,
With fierce gusts and precipitating force,
Through the white ridges of the chafed sea.
The waves arose. Higher and higher still
Their fierce necks writhed beneath the tempest's scourge
Like serpents struggling in a vulture's grasp.
Calm and rejoicing in the fearful war
Of wave running on wave, and blast on blast
Descending, and black flood on whirlpool driven
With dark obliterating course, he sate:
As if their genii were the ministers
Appointed to conduct him to the light
Of those beloved eyes, the Poet sate
Holding the steady helm. Evening came on,
The beams of sunset hung their rainbow hues
High 'mid the shifting domes of sheeted spray
That canopied his path o'er the waste deep;
Twilight, ascending slowly from the east,
Entwin'd in duskier wreaths her braided locks
O'er the fair front and radiant eyes of day;
Night followed, clad with stars. On every side
More horribly the multitudinous streams
Of ocean's mountainous waste to mutual war

Rushed in dark tumult thundering, as to mock
The calm and spangled sky. The little boat
Still fled before the storm; still fled, like foam
Down the steep cataract of a wintry river;
Now pausing on the edge of the riven wave;
Now leaving far behind the bursting mass
That fell, convulsing ocean. Safely fled—
As if that frail and wasted human form,
Had been an elemental god.
                                        At midnight
The moon arose: and lo! the ethereal cliffs
Of Caucasus, whose icy summits shone
Among the stars like sunlight, and around
Whose cavern'd base the whirlpools and the waves
Bursting and eddying irresistibly
Rage and resound forever—Who shall save?—
The boat fled on—the boiling torrent drove—
The crags closed round with black and jagged arms,
The shattered mountain overhung the sea,
And faster still, beyond all human speed,
Suspended on the sweep of the smooth wave,
The little boat was driven. A cavern there
Yawned, and amid its slant and winding depths
Engulfed the rushing sea. The boat fled on
With unrelaxing speed—"Vision and Love!"
The Poet cried aloud, "I have beheld
The path of thy departure. Sleep and death
Shall not divide us long!"

                              The boat pursued
The winding of the cavern. Daylight shone
At length upon that gloomy river's flow;
Now, where the fiercest war among the waves
Is calm, on the unfathomable stream
The boat moved slowly. Where the mountain, riven,
Exposed those black depths to the azure sky,

Ere yet the flood's enormous volume fell
Even to the base of Caucasus, with sound
That shook the everlasting rocks, the mass
Filled with one whirlpool all that ample chasm;
Stair above stair the eddying waters rose,
Circling immeasurably fast, and laved
With alternating dash the gnarled roots
Of mighty trees, that stretched their giant arms
In darkness over it. I' the midst was left,
Reflecting, yet distorting every cloud,
A pool of treacherous and tremendous calm.
Seized by the sway of the ascending stream,
With dizzy swiftness, round, and round, and round,
Ridge after ridge the straining boat arose,
Till on the verge of the extremest curve,
Where, through an opening of the rocky bank,
The waters overflow, and a smooth spot
Of glassy quiet mid those battling tides
Is left, the boat paused shuddering—Shall it sink
Down the abyss? Shall the reverting stress
Of that resistless gulf embosom it?
Now shall it fall?—A wandering stream of wind,
Breathed from the west, has caught the expanded sail,
And lo! with gentle motion, between banks
Of mossy slope, and on a placid stream,
Beneath a woven grove it sails, and, hark!
The ghastly torrent mingles its far roar,
With the breeze murmuring in the musical woods.
Where the embowering trees recede, and leave
A little space of green expanse, the cove
Is closed by meeting banks, whose yellow flowers
Forever gaze on their own drooping eyes,
Reflected in the crystal calm. The wave
Of the boat's motion marred their pensive task,
Which naught but vagrant bird, or wanton wind,
Or falling spear grass, or their own decay

Had e'er disturbed before. The Poet longed
To deck with their bright hues his withered hair,
But on his heart its solitude returned,
And he forbore. Not the strong impulse hid
In those flushed cheeks, bent eyes, and shadowy frame,
Had yet performed its ministry: it hung
Upon his life, as lightning in a cloud
Gleams, hovering ere it vanish, ere the floods
Of night close over it.
                          The noonday sun
Now shone upon the forest, one vast mass
Of mingling shade, whose brown magnificence
A narrow vale embosoms. There, huge caves,
Scooped in the dark base of their aery rocks
Mocking its moans, respond and roar forever.
The meeting boughs and implicated leaves
Wove twilight o'er the Poet's path, as led
By love, or dream, or god, or mightier Death,
He sought in Nature's dearest haunt, some bank,
Her cradle, and his sepulcher. More dark
And dark the shades accumulate. The oak,
Expanding its immense and knotty arms,
Embraces the light beech. The pyramids
Of the tall cedar overarching, frame
Most solemn domes within, and far below,
Like clouds suspended in an emerald sky,
The ash and the acacia floating hang
Tremulous and pale. Like restless serpents, clothed
In rainbow and in fire, the parasites,
Starred with ten thousand blossoms, flow around
The gray trunks, and, as gamesome infants' eyes,
With gentle meanings, and most innocent wiles,
Fold their beams round the hearts of those that love,
These twine their tendrils with the wedded boughs
Uniting their close union; the woven leaves
Make net-work of the dark blue light of day,

And the night's noontide clearness, mutable
As shapes in the weird clouds. Soft mossy lawns
Beneath these canopies extend their swells,
Fragrant with perfumed herbs, and eyed with blooms
Minute yet beautiful. One darkest glen
Sends from its woods of musk rose, twined with jasmine,
A soul-dissolving odor, to invite
To some more lovely mystery. Through the dell,
Silence and Twilight here, twin-sisters, keep
Their noonday watch, and sail among the shades,
Like vaporous shapes half seen; beyond, a well,
Dark, gleaming, and of most translucent wave,
Images all the woven boughs above,
And each depending leaf, and every speck
Of azure sky, darting between their chasms;
Nor aught else in the liquid mirror laves
Its portraiture, but some inconstant star
Between one foliaged lattice twinkling fair,
Or, painted bird, sleeping beneath the moon,
Or gorgeous insect floating motionless,
Unconscious of the day, ere yet his wings
Have spread their glories to the gaze of noon.

Hither the Poet came. His eyes beheld
Their own wan light through the reflected lines
Of his thin hair, distinct in the dark depth
Of that still fountain; as the human heart,
Gazing in dreams over the gloomy grave,
Sees its own treacherous likeness there. He heard
The motion of the leaves, the grass that sprung
Startled and glanced and trembled even to feel
An unaccustomed presence, and the sound
Of the sweet brook that from the secret springs
Of that dark fountain rose. A Spirit seemed
To stand beside him—clothed in no bright robes
Of shadowy silver or enshrining light,

Borrowed from aught the visible world affords
Of grace, or majesty, or mystery—
But, undulating woods, and silent well,
And leaping rivulet, and evening gloom
Now deepening the dark shades, for speech assuming
Held commune with him, as if he and it
Were all that was—only . . . when his regard
Was raised by intense pensiveness, . . . two eyes,
Two starry eyes, hung in the gloom of thought,
And seemed with their serene and azure smiles
To beckon him.

               Obedient to the light
That shone within his soul, he went, pursuing
The windings of the dell—The rivulet
Wanton and wild, through many a green ravine
Beneath the forest flowed. Sometimes it fell
Among the moss with hollow harmony
Dark and profound. Now on the polished stones
It danced; like childhood laughing as it went:
Then, through the plain in tranquil wanderings crept,
Reflecting every herb and drooping bud
That overhung its quietness—"O stream!
Whose source is inaccessibly profound,
Whither do thy mysterious waters tend?
Thou imagest my life. Thy darksome stillness,
Thy dazzling waves, thy loud and hollow gulfs,
Thy searchless fountain, and invisible course
Have each their type in me: and the wide sky,
And measureless ocean may declare as soon
What oozy cavern or what wandering cloud
Contains thy waters, as the universe
Tell where these living thoughts reside, when stretched
Upon thy flowers my bloodless limbs shall waste
I' the passing wind!"

Beside the grassy shore
Of the small stream he went; he did impress
On the green moss his tremulous step, that caught
Strong shuddering from his burning limbs. As one
Roused by some joyous madness from the couch
Of fever, he did move; yet, not like him,
Forgetful of the grave, where, when the flame
Of his frail exultation shall be spent,
He must descend. With rapid steps he went
Beneath the shade of trees, beside the flow
Of the wild babbling rivulet; and now
The forest's solemn canopies were changed
For the uniform and lightsome evening sky.
Gray rocks did peep from the spare moss, and stemmed
The struggling brook: tall spires of windlestrae
Threw their thin shadows down the rugged slope,
And naught but gnarled roots of antient pines
Branchless and blasted, clenched with grasping roots
The unwilling soil. A gradual change was here,
Yet ghastly. For, as fast years flow away,
The smooth brow gathers, and the hair grows thin
And white, and where irradiate dewy eyes
Had shone, gleam stony orbs—so from his steps
Bright flowers departed, and the beautiful shade
Of the green groves, with all their odorous winds
And musical motions. Calm, he still pursued
The stream, that with a larger volume now
Rolled through the labyrinthine dell; and there
Fretted a path through its descending curves
With its wintry speed. On every side now rose
Rocks, which, in unimaginable forms,
Lifted their black and barren pinnacles
In the light of evening, and its precipice
Obscuring the ravine, disclosed above,
Mid toppling stones, black gulfs and yawning caves,
Whose windings gave ten thousand various tongues

To the loud stream. Lo! where the pass expands
Its stony jaws, the abrupt mountain breaks,
And seems, with its accumulated crags,
To overhang the world: for wide expand
Beneath the wan stars and descending moon
Islanded seas, blue mountains, mighty streams,
Dim tracts and vast, robed in the lustrous gloom
Of leaden-colored even, and fiery hills
Mingling their flames with twilight, on the verge
Of the remote horizon. The near scene,
In naked and severe simplicity,
Made contrast with the universe. A pine,
Rock-rooted, stretched athwart the vacancy
Its swinging boughs, to each inconstant blast
Yielding one only response, at each pause
In most familiar cadence, with the howl
The thunder and the hiss of homeless streams
Mingling its solemn song, whilst the broad river,
Foaming and hurrying o'er its rugged path,
Fell into that immeasurable void
Scattering its waters to the passing winds.

    Yet the gray precipice and solemn pine
And torrent, were not all—one silent nook
Was there. Even on the edge of that vast mountain,
Upheld by knotty roots and fallen rocks,
It overlooked in its serenity
The dark earth, and the bending vault of stars.
It was a tranquil spot, that seemed to smile
Even in the lap of horror. Ivy clasped
The fissured stones with its entwining arms,
And did embower with leaves forever green,
And berries dark, the smooth and even space
Of its inviolated floor, and here
The children of the autumnal whirlwind bore,
In wanton sport, those bright leaves, whose decay,

Red, yellow, or ethereally pale,
Rivals the pride of summer. 'Tis the haunt
Of every gentle wind, whose breath can teach
The wilds to love tranquility. One step,
One human step alone, has ever broken
The stillness of its solitude—one voice
Alone inspired its echoes—even that voice
Which hither came, floating among the winds,
And led the loveliest among human forms
To make their wild haunts the depository
Of all the grace and beauty that endued
Its motions, render up its majesty,
Scatter its music on the unfeeling storm,
And to the damp leaves and blue cavern mold,
Nurses of rainbow flowers and branching moss,
Commit the colors of that varying cheek,
That snowy breast, those dark and drooping eyes.

The dim and horned moon hung low, and poured
A sea of luster on the horizon's verge
That overflowed its mountains. Yellow mist
Filled the unbounded atmosphere, and drank
Wan moonlight even to fullness: not a star
Shone, not a sound was heard; the very winds,
Danger's grim playmates, on that precipice
Slept, clasped in his embrace—O, storm of death!
Whose sightless speed divides this sullen night:
And thou, colossal Skeleton, that, still
Guiding its irresistible career
In thy devastating omnipotence,
Art king of this frail world, from the red field
Of slaughter, from the reeking hospital,
The patriot's sacred couch, the snowy bed
Of innocence, the scaffold and the throne,
A mighty voice invokes thee. Ruin calls
His brother Death. A rare and regal prey

He hath prepared, prowling around the world;
Glutted with which thou mayst repose, and men
Go to their graves like flowers or creeping worms,
Nor ever more offer at thy dark shrine
The unheeded tribute of a broken heart.

When on the threshold of the green recess
The wanderer's footsteps fell, he knew that death
Was on him. Yet a little, ere it fled,
Did he resign his high and holy soul
To images of the majestic past,
That paused within his passive being now,
Like winds that bear sweet music, when they breathe
Through some dim latticed chamber. He did place
His pale lean hand upon the rugged trunk
Of the old pine. Upon an ivied stone
Reclined his languid head, his limbs did rest,
Diffused and motionless, on the smooth brink
Of that obscurest chasm—and thus he lay,
Surrendering to their final impulses
The hovering powers of life. Hope and despair,
The torturers, slept; no mortal pain or fear
Marred his repose, the influxes of sense,
And his own being unalloyed by pain,
Yet feebler and more feeble, calmly fed
The stream of thought, till he lay breathing there
At peace, and faintly smiling—his last sight
Was the great moon, which o'er the western line
Of the wide world her mighty horn suspended,
With whose dun beams inwoven darkness seemed
To mingle. Now upon the jagged hills
It rests, and still as the divided frame
Of the vast meteor sunk, the Poet's blood,
That ever beat in mystic sympathy
With nature's ebb and flow, grew feebler still:
And when two lessening points of light alone

Gleamed through the darkness, the alternate gasp
Of his faint respiration scarce did stir
The stagnate night—till the minutest ray
Was quenched, the pulse yet lingered in his heart.
It paused—it fluttered. But when heaven remained
Utterly black, the murky shades involved
An image, silent, cold, and motionless,
As their own voiceless earth and vacant air.
Even as a vapor fed with golden beams
That ministered on sunlight, ere the west
Eclipses it, was now that wonderous frame—
No sense, no motion, no divinity—
A fragile lute, on whose harmonious strings
The breath of heaven did wander—a bright stream
Once fed with many-voiced waves—a dream
Of youth, which night and time have quenched forever,
Still, dark, and dry, and unremembered now.

O, for Medea's wondrous alchemy,
Which wheresoe'er it fell made the earth gleam
With bright flowers, and the wintry boughs exhale
From vernal blooms fresh fragrance! O, that God,
Profuse of poisons, would concede the chalice
Which but one living man has drained, who now,
Vessel of deathless wrath, a slave that feels
No proud exemption in the blighting curse
He bears, over the world wanders forever,
Lone as incarnate death! O, that the dream
Of dark magician in his visioned cave,
Raking the cinders of a crucible
For life and power, even when his feeble hand
Shakes in its last decay, were the true law
Of this so lovely world! But thou art fled
Like some frail exhalation; which the dawn
Robes in its golden beams—ah! thou hast fled!
The brave, the gentle, and the beautiful,

The child of grace and genius. Heartless things
Are done and said i' the world, and many worms
And beasts and men live on, and mighty Earth
From sea and mountain, city and wilderness,
In vesper low or joyous orison,
Lifts still its solemn voice—but thou art fled—
Thou canst no longer know or love the shapes
Of this phantasmal scene, who have to thee
Been purest ministers, who are, alas!
Now thou art not. Upon those pallid lips
So sweet even in their silence, on those eyes
That image sleep in death, upon that form
Yet safe from the worm's outrage, let no tear
Be shed—not even in thought. Nor, when those hues
Are gone, and those divinest lineaments,
Worn by the senseless wind, shall live alone
In the frail pauses of this simple strain,
Let not high verse, mourning the memory
Of that which is no more, or painting's woe
Or sculpture, speak in feeble imagery
Their own cold powers. Art and eloquence,
And all the shows o' the world are frail and vain
To weep a loss that turns their lights to shade.
It is a woe too "deep for tears," when all
Is reft at once, when some surpassing Spirit,
Whose light adorned the world around it, leaves
Those who remain behind, not sobs or groans,
The passionate tumult of a clinging hope;
But pale despair and cold tranquility,
Nature's vast frame, the web of human things,
Birth and the grave, that are not as they were.

Julian and Maddalo

A CONVERSATION

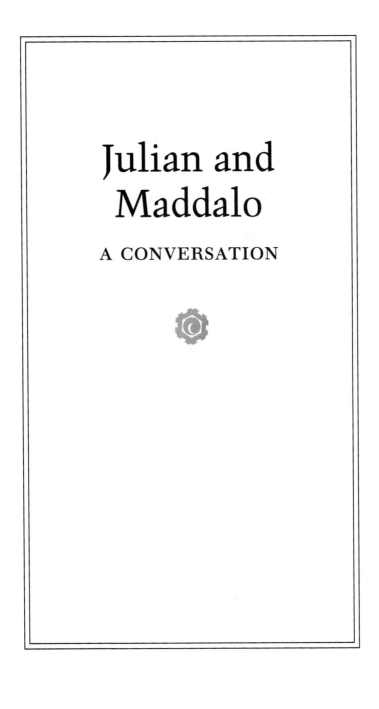

JULIAN AND MADDALO;

A CONVERSATION

The meadows with fresh streams, the bees with thyme,
The goats with the green leaves of budding spring,
Are saturated not—nor Love with tears.

Virgil's Gallus

Count Maddalo is a Venetian nobleman of ancient family and of great fortune, who, without mixing much in
the society of his countrymen, resides chiefly at his
magnificent palace in that city. He is a person of the
most consummate genius, and capable, if he would
direct his energies to such an end, of becoming the
redeemer of his degraded country. But it is his weakness to be proud: he derives, from a comparison of his
own extraordinary mind with the dwarfish intellects
that surround him, an intense apprehension of the
nothingness of human life. His passions and his powers
are incomparably greater than those of other men; and,
instead of the latter having been employed in curbing
the former, they have mutually lent each other strength.
His ambition preys upon itself, for want of objects
which it can consider worthy of exertion. I say that
Maddalo is proud, because I can find no other word to
express the concentered and impatient feelings which
consume him; but it is on his own hopes and affections
only that he seems to trample, for in social life no
human being can be more gentle, patient, and unas-
suming than Maddalo. He is cheerful, frank, and witty.
His more serious conversation is a sort of intoxication;
men are held by it as by a spell. He has traveled much;
and there is an inexpressible charm in his relation of
his adventures in different countries.

Julian is an Englishman of good family, passionately attached to those philosophical notions which assert the power of man over his own mind, and the immense improvements of which, by the extinction of certain moral superstitions, human society may be yet susceptible. Without concealing the evil in the world, he is forever speculating how good may be made superior. He is a complete infidel, and a scoffer at all things reputed holy; and Maddalo takes a wicked pleasure in drawing out his taunts against religion. What Maddalo thinks on these matters is not exactly known. Julian, in spite of his heterodox opinions, is conjectured by his friends to possess some good qualities. How far this is possible the pious reader will determine. Julian is rather serious.

Of the Maniac I can give no information. He seems by his own account to have been disappointed in love. He was evidently a very cultivated and amiable person when in his right senses. His story, told at length, might be like many other stories of the same kind: the unconnected exclamations of his agony will perhaps be found a sufficient comment for the text of every heart.

I rode one evening with Count Maddalo
Upon the bank of land which breaks the flow
Of Adria towards Venice—a bare strand
Of hillocks, heaped from ever-shifting sand,
Matted with thistles and amphibious weeds,
Such as from earth's embrace the salt ooze breeds,
Is this—an uninhabitable seaside
Which the lone fisher, when his nets are dried,
Abandons; and no other object breaks
The waste, but one dwarf tree and some few stakes
Broken and unrepaired, and the tide makes
A narrow space of level sand thereon—
Where 'twas our wont to ride while day went down.
This ride was my delight—I love all waste
And solitary places; where we taste
The pleasure of believing what we see
Is boundless, as we wish our souls to be:
And such was this wide ocean, and this shore
More barren than its billows—and yet more
Than all, with a remembered friend I love
To ride as then I rode—for the winds drove
The living spray along the sunny air
Into our faces; the blue heavens were bare,
Stripped to their depths by the awakening North;
And, from the waves, sound like delight broke forth
Harmonizing with solitude, and sent
Into our hearts aerial merriment . . .
So, as we rode, we talked; and the swift thought,
Winging itself with laughter, lingered not,
But flew from brain to brain—such glee was ours—
Charged with light memories of remembered hours,
None slow enough for sadness: till we came
Homeward, which always makes the spirit tame.
This day had been cheerful but cold, and now
The sun was sinking, and the wind also.
Our talk grew somewhat serious, as may be

Talk interrupted with such raillery
As mocks itself, because it cannot scorn
The thoughts it would extinguish—'twas forlorn
Yet pleasing, such as once, so poets tell,
The devils held within the dales of Hell
Concerning God, freewill and destiny:
Of all that earth has been or yet may be,
All that vain men imagine or believe,
Or hope can paint or suffering may achieve,
We descanted, and I (forever still
Is it not wise to make the best of ill?)
Argued against despondency, but pride
Made my companion take the darker side.
The sense that he was greater than his kind
Had struck, methinks, his eagle spirit blind
By gazing on its own exceeding light.
—Meanwhile the sun paused ere it should alight,
Over the horizon of the mountains—Oh,
How beautiful is sunset, when the glow
Of Heaven descends upon a land like thee,
Thou Paradise of exiles, Italy!
Thy mountains, seas and vineyards and the towers
Of cities they encircle!——it was ours
To stand on thee, beholding it; and then
Just where we had dismounted, the Count's men
Were waiting for us with the gondola—
As those who pause on some delightful way
Though bent on pleasant pilgrimage, we stood
Looking upon the evening and the flood
Which lay between the city and the shore
Paved with the image of the sky . . . the hoar
And aery Alps towards the North appeared
Through mist, an heaven-sustaining bulwark reared
Between the East and West; and half the sky
Was roofed with clouds of rich emblazonry
Dark purple at the zenith, which still grew

Down the steep West into a wondrous hue
Brighter than burning gold, even to the rent
Where the swift sun yet paused in his descent
Among the many folded hills: they were
Those famous Euganean hills, which bear
As seen from Lido through the harbor piles
The likeness of a clump of peaked isles—
And then—as if the Earth and Sea had been
Dissolved into one lake of fire, were seen
Those mountains towering as from waves of flame
Around the vaporous sun, from which there came
The inmost purple spirit of light, and made
Their very peaks transparent. "Ere it fade,"
Said my Companion, "I will show you soon
A better station"—so, o'er the lagoon
We glided, and from that funereal bark
I leaned, and saw the City, and could mark
How from their many isles, in evening's gleam,
Its temples and its palaces did seem
Like fabrics of enchantment piled to Heaven.
I was about to speak, when—"We are even
Now at the point I meant," said Maddalo,
And bade the gondolieri cease to row.
"Look, Julian, on the West, and listen well
If you hear not a deep and heavy bell."
I looked, and saw between us and the sun
A building on an island; such a one
As age to age might add, for uses vile,
A windowless, deformed and dreary pile;
And on the top an open tower, where hung
A bell, which in the radiance swayed and swung;
We could just hear its hoarse and iron tongue:
The broad sun sunk behind it, and it tolled
In strong and black relief—"What we behold
Shall be the madhouse and its belfry tower,"
Said Maddalo, "and ever at this hour

Those who may cross the water, hear that bell
Which calls the maniacs each one from his cell
To vespers."—"As much skill as need to pray
In thanks or hope for their dark lot have they
To their stern maker," I replied. "O ho!
You talk as in years past," said Maddalo.
"'Tis strange men change not. You were ever still
Among Christ's flock a perilous infidel,
A wolf for the meek lambs—if you can't swim
Beware of Providence." I looked on him,
But the gay smile had faded in his eye.
"And such"—he cried, "is our mortality
And this must be the emblem and the sign
Of what should be eternal and divine!—
And like that black and dreary bell, the soul,
Hung in a heaven-illumined tower, must toll
Our thoughts and our desires to meet below
Round the rent heart and pray—as madmen do
For what? they know not—till the night of death
As sunset that strange vision, severeth
Our memory from itself, and us from all
We sought and yet were baffled!" I recall
The sense of what he said, although I mar
The force of his expressions. The broad star
Of day meanwhile had sunk behind the hill
And the black bell became invisible
And the red tower looked gray, and all between
The churches, ships and palaces were seen
Huddled in gloom—into the purple sea
The orange hues of heaven sunk silently.
We hardly spoke, and soon the gondola
Conveyed me to my lodging by the way.

The following morn was rainy, cold and dim:
Ere Maddalo arose, I called on him,
And whilst I waited with his child I played;

A lovelier toy sweet Nature never made,
A serious, subtle, wild, yet gentle being,
Graceful without design and unforeseeing,
With eyes—oh speak not of her eyes!—which seem
Twin mirrors of Italian Heaven, yet gleam
With such deep meaning, as we never see
But in the human countenance: with me
She was a special favorite: I had nursed
Her fine and feeble limbs when she came first
To this bleak world; and she yet seemed to know
On second sight her antient playfellow,
Less changed than she was by six months or so;
For after her first shyness was worn out
We sate there, rolling billiard balls about.
When the Count entered—salutations past—
"The word you spoke last night might well have cast
A darkness on my spirit—if man be
The passive thing you say, I should not see
Much harm in the religions and old saws
(Though I may never own such leaden laws)
Which break a teachless nature to the yoke:
Mine is another faith"—thus much I spoke
And noting he replied not, added: "See
This lovely child, blithe, innocent and free;
She spends a happy time with little care
While we to such sick thoughts subjected are
As came on you last night—it is our will
That thus enchains us to permitted ill—
We might be otherwise—we might be all
We dream of happy, high, majestical.
Where is the love, beauty and truth we seek
But in our mind? and if we were not weak
Should we be less in deed than in desire?"
"Ay, if we were not weak—and we aspire
How vainly to be strong!" said Maddalo;
"You talk Utopia." "It remains to know,"

I then rejoined, "and those who try may find
How strong the chains are which our spirit bind;
Brittle perchance as straw . . . We are assured
Much may be conquered, much may be endured
Of what degrades and crushes us. We know
That we have power over ourselves to do
And suffer—what, we know not till we try;
But something nobler than to live and die—
So taught those kings of old philosophy
Who reigned, before Religion made men blind;
And those who suffer with their suffering kind
Yet feel their faith, religion." "My dear friend,"
Said Maddalo, "my judgment will not bend
To your opinion, though I think you might
Make such a system refutation-tight
As far as words go. I knew one like you
Who to this city came some months ago
With whom I argued in this sort, and he
Is now gone mad—and so he answered me—
Poor fellow! but if you would like to go
We'll visit him, and his wild talk will show
How vain are such aspiring theories."
"I hope to prove the induction otherwise,
And that a want of that true theory, still,
Which seeks a 'soul of goodness' in things ill
Or in himself or others has thus bowed
His being—there are some by nature proud,
Who patient in all else demand but this:
To love and be beloved with gentleness;
And being scorned, what wonder if they die
Some living death? this is not destiny
But man's own willful ill." As thus I spoke
Servants announced the gondola, and we
Through the last-falling rain and high-wrought sea
Sailed to the island where the madhouse stands.
We disembarked. The clap of tortured hands,

Fierce yells and howlings and lamentings keen,
And laughter where complaint had merrier been,
Moans, shrieks and curses and blaspheming prayers
Accosted us. We climbed the oozy stairs
Into an old courtyard. I heard on high,
Then, fragments of most touching melody,
But looking up saw not the singer there—
Through the black bars in the tempestuous air
I saw, like weeds on a wrecked palace growing,
Long tangled locks flung wildly forth, and flowing,
Of those who on a sudden were beguiled
Into strange silence, and looked forth and smiled
Hearing sweet sounds—Then I: "Methinks there were
A cure of these with patience and kind care,
If music can thus move . . . but what is he
Whom we seek here?" "Of his sad history
I know but this," said Maddalo: "he came
To Venice a dejected man, and fame
Said he was wealthy, or he had been so;
Some thought the loss of fortune wrought him woe;
But he was ever talking in such sort
As you do—far more sadly—he seemed hurt,
Even as a man with his peculiar wrong,
To hear but of the oppression of the strong,
Or those absurd deceits (I think with you
In some respects, you know) which carry through
The excellent impostors of this Earth
When they outface detection—he had worth,
Poor fellow! but a humorist in his way"—
"Alas, what drove him mad?" "I cannot say;
A Lady came with him from France, and when
She left him and returned, he wandered then
About yon lonely isles of desert sand
Till he grew wild—he had no cash or land
Remaining—the police had brought him here—
Some fancy took him and he would not bear

Removal; so I fitted up for him
Those rooms beside the sea, to please his whim,
And sent him busts and books and urns for flowers,
Which had adorned his life in happier hours,
And instruments of music—you may guess
A stranger could do little more or less
For one so gentle and unfortunate;
And those are his sweet strains which charm the weight
From madmen's chains, and make this Hell appear
A heaven of sacred silence, hushed to hear."—
"Nay, this was kind of you—he had no claim,
As the world says"—"None—but the very same
Which I on all mankind were I as he
Fallen to such deep reverse—his melody
Is interrupted now—we hear the din
Of madmen, shriek on shriek again begin;
Let us now visit him; after this strain
He ever communes with himself again,
And sees nor hears not any." Having said
These words we called the keeper, and he led
To an apartment opening on the sea—
There the poor wretch was sitting mournfully
Near a piano, his pale fingers twined
One with the other, and the ooze and wind
Rushed through an open casement, and did sway
His hair, and starred it with the brackish spray;
His head was leaning on a music book,
And he was muttering, and his lean limbs shook;
His lips were pressed against a folded leaf
In hue too beautiful for health, and grief
Smiled in their motions as they lay apart—
As one who wrought from his own fervid heart
The eloquence of passion, soon he raised
His sad meek face and eyes lustrous and glazed
And spoke—sometimes as one who wrote and thought
His words might move some heart that heeded not

If sent to distant lands; and then as one
Reproaching deeds never to be undone
With wondering self-compassion; then his speech
Was lost in grief, and then his words came each
Unmodulated, cold, expressionless;
But that from one jarred accent you might guess
It was despair made them so uniform:
And all the while the loud and gusty storm
Hissed through the window, and we stood behind
Stealing his accents from the envious wind
Unseen. I yet remember what he said
Distinctly: such impression his words made.

"Month after month," he cried, "to bear this load
And as a jade urged by the whip and goad
To drag life on, which like a heavy chain
Lengthens behind with many a link of pain!—
And not to speak my grief—O not to dare
To give a human voice to my despair,
But live and move, and wretched thing! smile on
As if I never went aside to groan
And wear this mask of falsehood even to those
Who are most dear—not for my own repose—
Alas, no scorn or pain or hate could be
So heavy as that falsehood is to me—
But that I cannot bear more altered faces
Than needs must be, more changed and cold embraces,
More misery, disappointment and mistrust
To own me for their father . . . Would the dust
Were covered in upon my body now!
That the life ceased to toil within my brow!
And then these thoughts would at the least be fled;
Let us not fear such pain can vex the dead.

"What Power delights to torture us? I know
That to myself I do not wholly owe

What now I suffer, though in part I may.
Alas, none strewed sweet flowers upon the way
Where wandering heedlessly, I met pale Pain
My shadow, which will leave me not again—
If I have erred, there was no joy in error,
But pain and insult and unrest and terror;
I have not as some do, bought penitence
With pleasure, and a dark yet sweet offense,
For then—if love and tenderness and truth
Had overlived hope's momentary youth,
My creed should have redeemed me from repenting;
But loathed scorn and outrage unrelenting
Met love excited by far other seeming
Until the end was gained . . . as one from dreaming
Of sweetest peace, I woke, and found my state
Such as it is——
        "O Thou, my spirit's mate
Who, for thou art compassionate and wise,
Wouldst pity me from thy most gentle eyes
If this sad writing thou shouldst ever see—
My secret groans must be unheard by thee,
Thou wouldst weep tears bitter as blood to know
Thy lost friend's incommunicable woe.

   "Ye few by whom my nature has been weighed
In friendship, let me not that name degrade
By placing on your hearts the secret load
Which crushes mine to dust. There is one road
To peace and that is truth, which follow ye!
Love sometimes leads astray to misery.
Yet think not though subdued—and I may well
Say that I am subdued—that the full Hell
Within me would infect the untainted breast
Of sacred nature with its own unrest;
As some perverted beings think to find
In scorn or hate a medicine for the mind

Which scorn or hate have wounded—O how vain!
The dagger heals not but may rend again. . . .
Believe that I am ever still the same
In creed as in resolve, and what may tame
My heart, must leave the understanding free
Or all would sink in this keen agony—
Nor dream that I will join the vulgar cry,
Or with my silence sanction tyranny,
Or seek a moment's shelter from my pain
In any madness which the world calls gain,
Ambition or revenge or thoughts as stern
As those which make me what I am, or turn
To avarice or misanthropy or lust. . . .
Heap on me soon, O grave, thy welcome dust!
Till then the dungeon may demand its prey,
And poverty and shame may meet and say—
Halting beside me on the public way—
'That love-devoted youth is ours—let's sit
Beside him—he may live some six months yet.'
Or the red scaffold, as our country bends,
May ask some willing victim, or ye friends
May fall under some sorrow which this heart
Or hand may share or vanquish or avert;
I am prepared: in truth with no proud joy
To do or suffer aught, as when a boy
I did devote to justice and to love
My nature, worthless now! . . .
                              "I must remove
A veil from my pent mind. 'Tis torn aside!
O, pallid as death's dedicated bride,
Thou mockery which art sitting by my side,
Am I not wan like thee? at the grave's call
I haste, invited to thy wedding ball
To greet the ghastly paramour, for whom
Thou hast deserted me . . . and made the tomb
Thy bridal bed . . . But I beside your feet

Will lie and watch ye from my winding sheet—
Thus . . . wide awake, though dead . . . yet stay, O stay!
Go not so soon—I know not what I say—
Hear but my reasons . . . I am mad, I fear,
My fancy is o'erwrought . . . thou art not here . . .
Pale art thou, 'tis most true . . . but thou art gone,
Thy work is finished . . . I am left alone!—

❀   ❀   ❀   ❀   ❀   ❀   ❀

"Nay, was it I who wooed thee to this breast
Which, like a serpent, thou envenomest
As in repayment of the warmth it lent?
Didst thou not seek me for thine own content?
Did not thy love awaken mine? I thought
That thou wert she who said, 'You kiss me not
Ever, I fear you do not love me now'—
In truth I loved even to my overthrow
Her, who would fain forget these words: but they
Cling to her mind, and cannot pass away.

❀   ❀   ❀   ❀   ❀   ❀   ❀

"You say that I am proud—that when I speak
My lip is tortured with the wrongs which break
The spirit it expresses . . . Never one
Humbled himself before, as I have done!
Even the instinctive worm on which we tread
Turns, though it wound not—then with prostrate head
Sinks in the dust and writhes like me—and dies?
No: wears a living death of agonies!
As the slow shadows of the pointed grass
Mark the eternal periods, his pangs pass
Slow, ever-moving—making moments be
As mine seem—each an immortality!

❀   ❀   ❀   ❀   ❀   ❀   ❀

"That you had never seen me—never heard
My voice, and more than all had ne'er endured

The deep pollution of my loathed embrace—
That your eyes ne'er had lied love in my face—
That, like some maniac monk, I had torn out
The nerves of manhood by their bleeding root
With mine own quivering fingers, so that ne'er
Our hearts had for a moment mingled there
To disunite in horror—these were not
With thee, like some suppressed and hideous thought
Which flits athwart our musings, but can find
No rest within a pure and gentle mind . . .
Thou sealedst them with many a bare broad word,
And cearedst my memory o'er them—for I heard
And can forget not . . . they were ministered
One after one, those curses. Mix them up
Like self-destroying poisons in one cup,
And they will make one blessing which thou ne'er
Didst imprecate for, on me—death.

❀   ❀   ❀   ❀   ❀   ❀   ❀

                                 "It were
A cruel punishment for one most cruel,
If such can love, to make that love the fuel
Of the mind's hell; hate, scorn, remorse, despair:
But *me*—whose heart a stranger's tear might wear
As water drops the sandy fountain-stone,
Who loved and pitied all things, and could moan
For woes which others hear not, and could see
The absent with the glance of fantasy,
And with the poor and trampled sit and weep,
Following the captive to his dungeon deep;
Me—who am as a nerve o'er which do creep
The else unfelt oppressions of this earth
And was to thee the flame upon thy hearth
When all beside was cold—that thou on me
Shouldst rain these plagues of blistering agony—
Such curses are from lips once eloquent

With love's too partial praise—let none relent
Who intend deeds too dreadful for a name
Henceforth, if an example for the same
They seek . . . for thou on me lookedst so, and so—
And didst speak thus . . . and thus . . . I live to show
How much men bear and die not!

    ✿   ✿   ✿   ✿   ✿   ✿   ✿

                                             "Thou wilt tell
With the grimace of hate how horrible
It was to meet my love when thine grew less;
Thou wilt admire how I could e'er address
Such features to love's work . . . this taunt, though true,
(For indeed nature nor in form nor hue
Bestowed on me her choicest workmanship)
Shall not be thy defense . . . for since thy lip
Met mine first, years long past, since thine eye kindled
With soft fire under mine, I have not dwindled
Nor changed in mind or body, or in aught
But as love changes what it loveth not
After long years and many trials.
                                  "How vain
Are words! I thought never to speak again,
Not even in secret—not to my own heart—
But from my lips the unwilling accents start
And from my pen the words flow as I write,
Dazzling my eyes with scalding tears . . . my sight
Is dim to see that charactered in vain
On this unfeeling leaf which burns the brain
And eats into it . . . blotting all things fair
And wise and good which time had written there.

    "Those who inflict must suffer, for they see
The work of their own hearts and this must be
Our chastisement or recompense—O child!
I would that thine were like to be more mild

For both our wretched sakes . . . for thine the most
Who feelest already all that thou hast lost
Without the power to wish it thine again;
And as slow years pass, a funereal train
Each with the ghost of some lost hope or friend
Following it like its shadow, wilt thou bend
No thought on my dead memory?

    ✿   ✿   ✿   ✿   ✿   ✿   ✿

                                       "Alas, love,
Fear me not . . . against thee I would not move
A finger in despite. Do I not live
That thou mayst have less bitter cause to grieve?
I give thee tears for scorn and love for hate,
And that thy lot may be less desolate
Than his on whom thou tramplest, I refrain
From that sweet sleep which medicines all pain.
Then, when thou speakest of me, never say,
'He could forgive not.' Here I cast away
All human passions, all revenge, all pride;
I think, speak, act no ill; I do but hide
Under these words like embers, every spark
Of that which has consumed me—quick and dark
The grave is yawning . . . as its roof shall cover
My limbs with dust and worms under and over
So let Oblivion hide this grief . . . the air
Closes upon my accents, as despair
Upon my heart—let death upon despair!"

He ceased, and overcome leant back awhile,
Then rising, with a melancholy smile
Went to a sofa, and lay down, and slept
A heavy sleep, and in his dreams he wept
And muttered some familiar name, and we
Wept without shame in his society.
I think I never was impressed so much;

The man who were not, must have lacked a touch
Of human nature . . . then we lingered not,
Although our argument was quite forgot,
But calling the attendants, went to dine
At Maddalo's; yet neither cheer nor wine
Could give us spirits, for we talked of him
And nothing else, till daylight made stars dim;
And we agreed his was some dreadful ill
Wrought on him boldly, yet unspeakable
By a dear friend; some deadly change in love
Of one vowed deeply which he dreamed not of;
For whose sake he, it seemed, had fixed a blot
Of falsehood on his mind which flourished not
But in the light of all-beholding truth;
And having stamped this canker on his youth
She had abandoned him—and how much more
Might be his woe, we guessed not—he had store
Of friends and fortune once, as we could guess
From his nice habits and his gentleness;
These were now lost . . . it were a grief indeed
If he had changed one unsustaining reed
For all that such a man might else adorn.
The colors of his mind seemed yet unworn;
For the wild language of his grief was high,
Such as in measure were called poetry;
And I remember one remark which then
Maddalo made. He said: "Most wretched men
Are cradled into poetry by wrong,
They learn in suffering what they teach in song."

If I had been an unconnected man
I, from this moment, should have formed some plan
Never to leave sweet Venice—for to me
It was delight to ride by the lone sea;
And then, the town is silent—one may write
Or read in gondolas by day or night,

Having the little brazen lamp alight,
Unseen, uninterrupted; books are there,
Pictures, and casts from all those statues fair
Which were twin-born with poetry, and all
We seek in towns, with little to recall
Regrets for the green country. I might sit
In Maddalo's great palace, and his wit
And subtle talk would cheer the winter night
And make me know myself, and the firelight
Would flash upon our faces, till the day
Might dawn and make me wonder at my stay:
But I had friends in London too: the chief
Attraction here, was that I sought relief
From the deep tenderness that maniac wrought
Within me—'twas perhaps an idle thought,
But I imagined that if day by day
I watched him, and but seldom went away,
And studied all the beatings of his heart
With zeal, as men study some stubborn art
For their own good, and could by patience find
An entrance to the caverns of his mind,
I might reclaim him from his dark estate:
In friendships I had been most fortunate—
Yet never saw I one whom I would call
More willingly my friend; and this was all
Accomplished not; such dreams of baseless good
Oft come and go in crowds or solitude
And leave no trace—but what I now designed
Made for long years impression on my mind.
The following morning, urged by my affairs,
I left bright Venice.

         After many years
And many changes I returned; the name
Of Venice, and its aspect, was the same;
But Maddalo was traveling far away

Among the mountains of Armenia.
His dog was dead. His child had now become
A woman; such as it has been my doom
To meet with few, a wonder of this earth,
Where there is little of transcendent worth,
Like one of Shakespeare's women: kindly she
And with a manner beyond courtesy
Received her father's friend; and when I asked
Of the lorn maniac, she her memory tasked
And told as she had heard the mournful tale:
"That the poor sufferer's health began to fail
Two years from my departure, but that then
The Lady who had left him, came again.
Her mien had been imperious, but she now
Looked meek—perhaps remorse had brought her low.
Her coming made him better, and they stayed
Together at my father's—for I played
As I remember with the lady's shawl—
I might be six years old—but after all
She left him" . . . "Why, her heart must have been tough:
How did it end?" "And was not this enough?
They met—they parted"—"Child, is there no more?"
"Something within that interval which bore
The stamp of *why* they parted, *how* they met:
Yet if thine aged eyes disdain to wet
Those wrinkled cheeks with youth's remembered tears,
Ask me no more, but let the silent years
Be closed and ceared over their memory
As yon mute marble where their corpses lie."
I urged and questioned still, she told me how
All happened—but the cold world shall not know.

From

Prometheus Unbound

A LYRICAL DRAMA

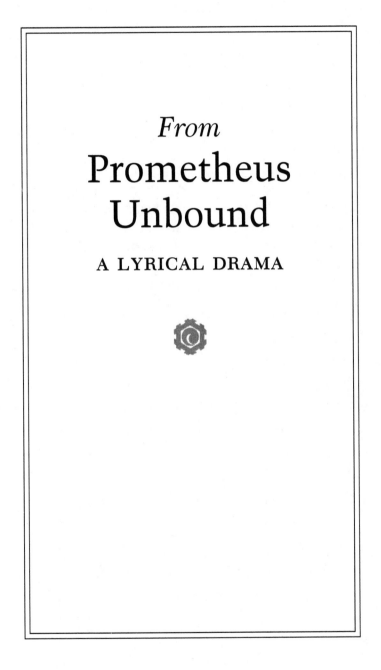

Dramatis Personae

PROMETHEUS

DEMOGORGON

JUPITER

THE EARTH

OCEAN

APOLLO

MERCURY

ASIA

PANTHEA } *Oceanides*

IONE

HERCULES

THE PHANTASM OF JUPITER

THE SPIRIT OF THE EARTH

THE SPIRIT OF THE MOON

SPIRITS OF THE HOURS

SPIRITS

ECHOES

FAUNS

FURIES

From
PROMETHEUS UNBOUND

From ACT I

Scene: A Ravine of Icy Rocks in the Indian Caucasus.
Prometheus is discovered bound to the Precipice.
Panthea and Ione are seated at his feet. Time, Night.
During the Scene, Morning slowly breaks.

PROMETHEUS

Monarch of Gods and Daemons, and all Spirits
But One, who throng those bright and rolling Worlds
Which Thou and I alone of living things
Behold with sleepless eyes! regard this Earth
Made multitudinous with thy slaves, whom thou
Requitest for knee-worship, prayer and praise,
And toil, and hecatombs of broken hearts,
With fear and self contempt and barren hope;
Whilst me, who am thy foe, eyeless in hate,
Hast thou made reign and triumph, to thy scorn,
O'er mine own misery and thy vain revenge—
Three thousand years of sleep-unsheltered hours
And moments—aye divided by keen pangs
Till they seemed years, torture and solitude,
Scorn and despair—these are mine empire—
More glorious far than that which thou surveyest
From thine unenvied throne, O Mighty God!
Almighty, had I deigned to share the shame
Of thine ill tyranny, and hung not here
Nailed to this wall of eagle-baffling mountain,
Black, wintry, dead, unmeasured; without herb,
Insect, or beast, or shape or sound of life.
Ah me, alas, pain, pain ever, forever!
No change, no pause, no hope!—Yet I endure.

I ask the Earth, have not the mountains felt?
I ask yon Heaven—the all-beholding Sun,
Has it not seen? The Sea, in storm or calm,
Heaven's ever-changing Shadow, spread below—
Have its deaf waves not heard my agony?
Ah me, alas, pain, pain ever, forever!

The crawling glaciers pierce me with the spears
Of their moon-freezing crystals; the bright chains
Eat with their burning cold into my bones.
Heaven's winged hound, polluting from thy lips
His beak in poison not his own, tears up
My heart; and shapeless sights come wandering by,
The ghastly people of the realm of dream,
Mocking me: and the Earthquake-fiends are charged
To wrench the rivets from my quivering wounds
When the rocks split and close again behind;
While from their loud abysses howling throng
The genii of the storm, urging the rage
Of whirlwind, and afflict me with keen hail.
And yet to me welcome is Day and Night,
Whether one breaks the hoarfrost of the morn,
Or starry, dim, and slow, the other climbs
The leaden-colored East; for then they lead
Their wingless, crawling Hours, one among whom
—As some dark Priest hales the reluctant victim—
Shall drag thee, cruel King, to kiss the blood
From these pale feet, which then might trample thee
If they disdained not such a prostrate slave.
Disdain? Ah no! I pity thee—What Ruin
Will hunt thee undefended through wide Heaven!
How will thy soul, cloven to its depth with terror,
Gape like a Hell within! I speak in grief,
Not exultation, for I hate no more,
As then, ere misery made me wise—The Curse
Once breathed on thee I would recall. Ye Mountains,

Whose many-voiced Echoes, through the mist
Of cataracts, flung the thunder of that spell!
Ye icy Springs, stagnant with wrinkling frost
Which vibrated to hear me, and then crept
Shuddering through India! Thou serenest Air,
Through which the Sun walks burning without beams!
And ye swift Whirlwinds, who on poised wings
Hung mute and moveless o'er yon hushed abyss,
As thunder louder than your own made rock
The orbed world! If then my words had power
—Though I am changed so that aught evil wish
Is dead within, although no memory be
Of what is hate—let them not lose it now!
What was that curse? for ye all heard me speak.

❖   ❖   ❖   ❖   ❖   ❖   ❖

PHANTASM

Fiend, I defy thee! with a calm, fixed mind,
   All that thou canst inflict I bid thee do;
Foul Tyrant both of Gods and Humankind,
   One only being shalt thou not subdue.
      Rain then thy plagues upon me here,
      Ghastly disease and frenzying fear;
      And let alternate frost and fire
      Eat into me, and be thine ire
Lightning and cutting hail and legioned forms
Of furies, driving by upon the wounding storms.

Aye, do thy worst. Thou art Omnipotent.
   O'er all things but thyself I gave thee power,
And my own will. Be thy swift mischiefs sent
   To blast mankind, from yon etherial tower.
      Let thy malignant spirit move
      Its darkness over those I love:
      On me and mine I imprecate
      The utmost torture of thy hate

And thus devote to sleepless agony
This undeclining head while thou must reign on high.

But thou who art the God and Lord—O thou
  Who fillest with thy soul this world of woe,
To whom all things of Earth and Heaven do bow
  In fear and worship—all-prevailing foe!
    I curse thee! let a sufferer's curse
    Clasp thee, his torturer, like remorse,
    Till thine Infinity shall be
    A robe of envenomed agony;
And thine Omnipotence a crown of pain
To cling like burning gold round thy dissolving brain.

Heap on thy soul by virtue of this Curse
  Ill deeds, then be thou damned, beholding good,
Both infinite as is the Universe,
  And thou, and thy self-torturing solitude.
    An awful Image of calm power
    Though now thou sittest, let the hour
    Come, when thou must appear to be
    That which thou art internally.
And after many a false and fruitless crime
Scorn track thy lagging fall through boundless space and time.
                    [*The Phantasm vanishes.*]

PROMETHEUS

Were these my words, O Parent?

THE EARTH

                    They were thine.

PROMETHEUS

  It doth repent me: words are quick and vain;
Grief for awhile is blind, and so was mine.
  I wish no living thing to suffer pain.

THE EARTH

Misery, O misery to me,
That Jove at length should vanquish thee.
Wail, howl aloud, Land and Sea,
The Earth's rent heart shall answer ye.
Howl, Spirits of the living and the dead,
Your refuge, your defense lies fallen and vanquished.

FIRST ECHO

Lies fallen and vanquished?

SECOND ECHO

Fallen and vanquished!

IONE

Fear not—'tis but some passing spasm,
The Titan is unvanquished still.

    ✿   ✿   ✿   ✿   ✿   ✿   ✿

FURY

Behold, an emblem—those who do endure
Deep wrongs for man, and scorn and chains, but heap
Thousand-fold torment on themselves and him.

PROMETHEUS

Remit the anguish of that lighted stare—
Close those wan lips—let that thorn-wounded brow
Stream not with blood—it mingles with thy tears!
Fix, fix those tortured orbs in peace and death
So thy sick throes shake not that crucifix,
So those pale fingers play not with thy gore—
O horrible! Thy name I will not speak,
It hath become a curse. I see, I see
The wise, the mild, the lofty and the just,

Whom thy slaves hate for being like to thee,
Some hunted by foul lies from their heart's home,
An early-chosen, late-lamented home,
As hooded ounces cling to the driven hind,
Some linked to corpses in unwholesome cells:
Some—hear I not the multitude laugh loud?—
Impaled in lingering fire: and mighty realms
Float by my feet like sea-uprooted isles
Whose sons are kneaded down in common blood
By the red light of their own burning homes.

FURY

Blood thou canst see, and fire; and canst hear groans;
Worse things, unheard, unseen, remain behind.

PROMETHEUS

Worse?

FURY

In each human heart terror survives
The ravine it has gorged: the loftiest fear
All that they would disdain to think were true:
Hypocrisy and custom make their minds
The fanes of many a worship, now outworn.
They dare not devise good for man's estate
And yet they know not that they do not dare.
The good want power, but to weep barren tears.
The powerful goodness want: worse need for them.
The wise want love, and those who love want wisdom;
And all best things are thus confused to ill.
Many are strong and rich—and would be just—
But live among their suffering fellow men
As if none felt: they know not what they do.

PROMETHEUS

Thy words are like a cloud of winged snakes
And yet, I pity those they torture not.

FURY

Thou pitiest them? I speak no more!

[Vanishes.]

PROMETHEUS

Ah woe!
Ah woe! Alas! pain, pain ever, forever!
I close my tearless eyes, but see more clear
Thy works within my woe-illumed mind,
Thou subtle Tyrant! . . . Peace is in the grave—
The grave hides all things beautiful and good—
I am a God and cannot find it there,
Nor would I seek it: for, though dread revenge,
This is defeat, fierce King, not victory.
The sights with which thou torturest gird my soul
With new endurance, till the hour arrives
When they shall be no types of things which are.

PANTHEA

Alas! what sawest thou?

PROMETHEUS

There are two woes:
To speak and to behold; thou spare me one.
Names are there, Nature's sacred watchwords—they
Were borne aloft in bright emblazonry.
The nations thronged around, and cried aloud
As with one voice, "Truth, liberty and love!"
Suddenly fierce confusion fell from Heaven
Among them—there was strife, deceit and fear;

Tyrants rushed in, and did divide the spoil.
This was the shadow of the truth I saw.

THE EARTH

I felt thy torture, Son, with such mixed joy
As pain and Virtue give—To cheer thy state
I bid ascend those subtle and fair spirits
Whose homes are the dim caves of human thought
And who inhabit, as birds wing the wind,
Its world-surrounding ether; they behold
Beyond that twilight realm, as in a glass,
The future—may they speak comfort to thee!

    ✿   ✿   ✿   ✿   ✿   ✿   ✿

CHORUS OF SPIRITS

From unremembered ages we
Gentle guides and guardians be
Of Heaven-oppressed mortality—
And we breathe, and sicken not,
The atmosphere of human thought:
Be it dim and dank and gray
Like a storm-extinguished day
Traveled o'er by dying gleams;
   Be it bright as all between
Cloudless skies and windless streams,
   Silent, liquid and serene—
As the birds within the wind,
   As the fish within the wave,
As the thoughts of man's own mind
   Float through all above the grave,
We make there, our liquid lair,
Voyaging cloudlike and unpent
Through the boundless element—
Thence we bear the prophecy
Which begins and ends in thee!

IONE

More yet come, one by one: the air around them
Looks radiant as the air around a star.

FIRST SPIRIT

On a battle trumpet's blast
I fled hither, fast, fast, fast,
Mid the darkness upward cast—
From the dust of creeds outworn,
From the tyrant's banner torn,
Gathering round me, onward borne,
There was mingled many a cry—
Freedom! Hope! Death! Victory!
Till they faded through the sky
And one sound above, around,
One sound beneath, around, above,
Was moving; 'twas the soul of love;
'Twas the hope, the prophecy,
Which begins and ends in thee.

SECOND SPIRIT

A rainbow's arch stood on the sea,
Which rocked beneath, immovably;
And the triumphant storm did flee,
Like a conqueror swift and proud
Between, with many a captive cloud
A shapeless, dark and rapid crowd,
Each by lightning riven in half—
I heard the thunder hoarsely laugh—
Mighty fleets were strewn like chaff
And spread beneath, a hell of death
O'er the white waters, I alit
On a great ship lightning-split
And speeded hither on the sigh
Of one who gave an enemy
His plank—then plunged aside to die.

THIRD SPIRIT

I sate beside a sage's bed
And the lamp was burning red
Near the book where he had fed,
When a Dream with plumes of flame
To his pillow hovering came,
And I knew it was the same
Which had kindled long ago
Pity, eloquence and woe;
And the world awhile below
Wore the shade its luster made.
It has borne me here as fleet
As Desire's lightning feet:
I must ride it back ere morrow,
Or the sage will wake in sorrow.

FOURTH SPIRIT

On a Poet's lips I slept
Dreaming like a love-adept
In the sound his breathing kept;
Nor seeks nor finds he mortal blisses
But feeds on the aerial kisses
Of shapes that haunt thought's wildernesses.
He will watch from dawn to gloom
The lake-reflected sun illume
The yellow bees i' the ivy-bloom
Nor heed nor see, what things they be;
But from these create he can
Forms more real than living man,
Nurslings of immortality!—
One of these awakened me
And I sped to succor thee.

❖   ❖   ❖   ❖   ❖   ❖   ❖

From ACT II

A *Forest, intermingled with Rocks and Caverns.* Asia and Panthea *pass into it. Two young Fauns are sitting on a Rock, listening.*

SEMICHORUS I OF SPIRITS

The path through which that lovely twain
　　Have past, by cedar, pine and yew?
　　And each dark tree that ever grew
　　Is curtained out from Heaven's wide blue;
Nor sun nor moon nor wind nor rain
　　　Can pierce its interwoven bowers;
　　Nor aught save when some cloud of dew,
Drifted along the earth-creeping breeze
Between the trunks of the hoar trees,
　　　Hangs each a pearl in the pale flowers
　　Of the green laurel, blown anew;
And bends and then fades silently
One frail and fair anemone;
Or when some star of many a one
That climbs and wanders through steep night,
Has found the cleft through which alone
Beams fall from high those depths upon,
Ere it is borne away, away,
By the swift Heavens that cannot stay—
It scatters drops of golden light
Like lines of rain that ne'er unite;
And the gloom divine is all around
And underneath is the mossy ground.

SEMICHORUS II

There the voluptuous nightingales
　　Are awake through all the broad noonday.

When one with bliss or sadness fails—
    And through the windless ivy-boughs,
    Sick with sweet love, droops dying away
On its mate's music-panting bosom—
Another from the swinging blossom,
        Watching to catch the languid close
    Of the last strain, then lifts on high
    The wings of the weak melody,
Till some new strain of feeling bear
    The song, and all the woods are mute;
When there is heard through the dim air
The rush of wings, and rising there
    Like many a lake-surrounded flute,
Sounds overflow the listener's brain
So sweet that joy is almost pain.

   ❋   ❋   ❋   ❋   ❋   ❋   ❋

SONG OF SPIRITS

To the Deep, to the Deep,
        Down, down!
Through the shade of Sleep,
Through the cloudy strife
Of Death and of Life;
Through the veil and the bar
Of things which seem and are,
Even to the steps of the remotest Throne,
        Down, down!

While the sound, whirls around,
        Down, down!
As the fawn draws the hound,
As the lightning the vapor,
As a weak moth the taper;
Death, Despair; Love, Sorrow;
Time both; today, tomorrow;
As steel obeys the Spirit of the stone,
        Down, down!

Through the gray, void Abysm,
                    Down, down!
Where the air is no prism
And the moon and stars are not
And the cavern crags wear not
The radiance of Heaven,
Nor the gloom to Earth given;
Where there is One pervading, One alone,
                    Down, down!

In the depth of the Deep,
                    Down, down!
Like veil'd Lightning asleep,
Like the spark nursed in embers,
The last look Love remembers,
Like a diamond which shines
On the dark wealth of mines,
A spell is treasured but for thee alone.
                    Down, down!

We have bound thee, we guide thee
                    Down, down!
With the bright form beside thee—
Resist not the weakness—
Such strength is in meekness—
That the Eternal, the Immortal,
Must unloose through life's portal
The snakelike Doom coiled underneath his throne
                    By that alone!

SCENE IV

The Cave of Demogorgon. Asia *and* Panthea.

PANTHEA

What veiled form sits on that ebon throne?

ASIA

The veil has fallen! . . .

PANTHEA

            I see a mighty Darkness
Filling the seat of power; and rays of gloom
Dart round, as light from the meridian Sun,
Ungazed upon and shapeless—neither limb
Nor form—nor outline; yet we feel it is
A living Spirit.

DEMOGORGON

Ask what thou wouldst know.

ASIA

What canst thou tell?

DEMOGORGON

          All things thou dar'st demand.

ASIA

Who made the living world?

DEMOGORGON

          God.

ASIA

             Who made all
That it contains—thought, passion, reason, will,
Imagination?

Demogorgon

God, Almighty God.

ASIA

Who made that sense which, when the winds of Spring
In rarest visitation, or the voice
Of one beloved heard in youth alone,
Fills the faint eyes with falling tears, which dim
The radiant looks of unbewailing flowers,
And leaves this peopled earth a solitude
When it returns no more?

DEMOGORGON

Merciful God.

ASIA

And who made terror, madness, crime, remorse,
Which from the links of the great chain of things
To every thought within the mind of man
Sway and drag heavily—and each one reels
Under the load towards the pit of death;
Abandoned hope, and love that turns to hate;
And self-contempt, bitterer to drink than blood;
Pain whose unheeded and familiar speech
Is howling and keen shrieks, day after day;
And Hell, or the sharp fear of Hell?

DEMOGORGON

He reigns.

ASIA

Utter his name—a world pining in pain
Asks but his name; curses shall drag him down.

DEMOGORGON

He reigns.

ASIA

I feel, I know it—who?

DEMOGORGON

He reigns.

ASIA

Who reigns? There was the Heaven and Earth at first
And Light and Love—then Saturn, from whose throne
Time fell, an envious shadow; such the state
Of the earth's primal spirits beneath his sway
As the calm joy of flowers and living leaves
Before the wind or sun has withered them
And semivital worms; but he refused
The birthright of their being, knowledge, power,
The skill which wields the elements, the thought
Which pierces this dim Universe like light,
Self-empire and the majesty of love,
For thirst of which they fainted. Then Prometheus
Gave wisdom, which is strength, to Jupiter
And with this law alone: "Let man be free,"
Clothed him with the dominion of wide Heaven.
To know nor faith nor love nor law, to be
Omnipotent but friendless, is to reign;
And Jove now reigned; for on the race of man
First famine and then toil and then disease,
Strife, wounds, and ghastly death unseen before,
Fell; and the unseasonable seasons drove,
With alternating shafts of frost and fire,
Their shelterless, pale tribes to mountain caves;
And in their desert hearts fierce wants he sent
And mad disquietudes, and shadows idle
Of unreal good, which levied mutual war,
So ruining the lair wherein they raged.
Prometheus saw, and waked the legioned hopes

Which sleep within folded Elysian flowers,
Nepenthe, Moly, Amaranth, fadeless blooms,
That they might hide with thin and rainbow wings
The shape of Death; and Love he sent to bind
The disunited tendrils of that vine
Which bears the wine of life, the human heart;
And he tamed fire, which like some beast of prey
Most terrible, but lovely, played beneath
The frown of man, and tortured to his will
Iron and gold, the slaves and signs of power,
And gems and poisons, and all subtlest forms
Hidden beneath the mountains and the waves.
He gave man speech, and speech created thought,
Which is the measure of the Universe;
And Science struck the thrones of Earth and Heaven
Which shook but fell not; and the harmonious mind
Poured itself forth in all-prophetic song,
And music lifted up the listening spirit
Until it walked, exempt from mortal care,
Godlike, o'er the clear billows of sweet sound;
And human hands first mimicked and then mocked
With molded limbs more lovely than its own
The human form, till marble grew divine,
And mothers, gazing, drank the love men see
Reflected in their race, behold, and perish.
He told the hidden power of herbs and springs,
And Disease drank and slept—Death grew like sleep—
He taught the implicated orbits woven
Of the wide-wandering stars, and how the Sun
Changes his lair, and by what secret spell
The pale moon is transformed, when her broad eye
Gazes not on the interlunar sea;
He taught to rule, as life directs the limbs,
The tempest-winged chariots of the Ocean,
And the Celt knew the Indian. Cities then
Were built, and through their snowlike columns flowed

The warm winds, and the azure ether shone,
And the blue sea and shadowy hills were seen . . .
Such the alleviations of his state
Prometheus gave to man—for which he hangs
Withering in destined pain—but who rains down
Evil, the immedicable plague, which while
Man looks on his creation like a God
And sees that it is glorious, drives him on,
The wreck of his own will, the scorn of Earth,
The outcast, the abandoned, the alone?—
Not Jove: while yet his frown shook Heaven, aye when
His adversary from adamantine chains
Cursed him, he trembled like a slave. Declare
Who is his master? Is he too a slave?

DEMOGORGON

All spirits are enslaved who serve things evil:
Thou knowest if Jupiter be such or no.

ASIA

Whom calledst thou God?

DEMOGORGON

            I spoke but as ye speak—
For Jove is the supreme of living things.

ASIA

Who is the master of the slave?

DEMOGORGON

            —If the Abysm
Could vomit forth its secrets—but a voice
Is wanting, the deep truth is imageless;
For what would it avail to bid thee gaze

On the revolving world? what to bid speak
Fate, Time, Occasion, Chance and Change? To these
All things are subject but eternal Love.

ASIA

So much I asked before, and my heart gave
The response thou hast given; and of such truths
Each to itself must be the oracle—
One more demand . . . and do thou answer me
As my own soul would answer, did it know
That which I ask—Prometheus shall arise
Henceforth the Sun of this rejoicing world:
When shall the destined hour arrive?

DEMOGORGON

Behold!

ASIA

The rocks are cloven, and through the purple night
I see Cars drawn by rainbow-winged steeds
Which trample the dim winds—in each there stands
A wild-eyed charioteer, urging their flight.
Some look behind, as fiends pursued them there
And yet I see no shapes but the keen stars:
Others with burning eyes lean forth, and drink
With eager lips the wind of their own speed
As if the thing they loved fled on before,
And now—even now they clasped it; their bright locks
Stream like a comet's flashing hair: they all
Sweep onward—

DEMOGORGON

These are the immortal Hours
Of whom thou didst demand—One waits for thee.

ASIA

A Spirit with a dreadful countenance
Checks its dark chariot by the craggy gulf.
Unlike thy brethren, ghastly charioteer,
What art thou? whither wouldst thou bear me? Speak!

SPIRIT

I am the shadow of a destiny
More dread than is mine aspect—ere yon planet
Has set, the Darkness which ascends with me
Shall wrap in lasting night Heaven's kingless throne.

ASIA

What meanest thou?

PANTHEA

    That terrible shadow floats
Up from its throne, as may the lurid smoke
Of earthquake-ruined cities o'er the sea—
Lo! it ascends the Car . . . the coursers fly
Terrified; watch its path among the stars
Blackening the night!

ASIA

    Thus I am answered—strange!

PANTHEA

See, near the verge another chariot stays;
An ivory shell inlaid with crimson fire
Which comes and goes within its sculptured rim
Of delicate strange tracery—the young Spirit
That guides it, has the dovelike eyes of hope.
How its soft smiles attract the soul!—as light
Lures winged insects through the lampless air.

SPIRIT

My coursers are fed with the lightning,
   They drink of the whirlwind's stream
And when the red morning is brightning
   They bathe in the fresh sunbeam;
     They have strength for their swiftness, I deem:
      Then ascend with me, daughter of Ocean.

I desire—and their speed makes night kindle;
   I fear—they outstrip the Typhoon;
Ere the cloud piled on Atlas can dwindle
   We encircle the earth and the moon:
     We shall rest from long labors at noon:
      Then ascend with me, daughter of Ocean.

SCENE V

The Car pauses within a Cloud on the Top of a snowy Mountain. Asia, Panthea *and the* Spirit of the Hour.

SPIRIT

On the brink of the night and the morning
   My coursers are wont to respire,
But the Earth has just whispered a warning
   That their flight must be swifter than fire:
   They shall drink the hot speed of desire!

ASIA

Thou breathest on their nostrils—but my breath
Would give them swifter speed.

SPIRIT

         Alas, it could not.

PANTHEA

O Spirit! pause and tell whence is the light
Which fills the cloud? the sun is yet unrisen.

SPIRIT

The sun will rise not until noon—Apollo
Is held in Heaven by wonder—and the light
Which fills this vapor, as the aerial hue
Of fountain-gazing roses fills the water,
Flows from thy mighty sister.

PANTHEA

                              Yes, I feel . . .

ASIA

What is it with thee, sister? Thou art pale.

PANTHEA

How thou art changed! I dare not look on thee;
I feel, but see thee not. I scarce endure
The radiance of thy beauty. Some good change
Is working in the elements which suffer
Thy presence thus unveiled—The Nereids tell
That on the day when the clear hyaline
Was cloven at thy uprise, and thou didst stand
Within a veined shell, which floated on
Over the calm floor of the crystal sea,
Among the Aegean isles, and by the shores
Which bear thy name, love, like the atmosphere
Of the sun's fire filling the living world,
Burst from thee, and illumined Earth and Heaven
And the deep ocean and the sunless caves,
And all that dwells within them; till grief cast
Eclipse upon the soul from which it came:

Such art thou now, nor is it I alone,
Thy sister, thy companion, thine own chosen one,
But the whole world which seeks thy sympathy.
Hearest thou not sounds i' the air which speak the love
Of all articulate beings? Feelest thou not
The inanimate winds enamored of thee?—List!

[Music.]

ASIA

Thy words are sweeter than aught else but his
Whose echoes they are—yet all love is sweet,
Given or returned; common as light is love
And its familiar voice wearies not ever.
Like the wide Heaven, the all-sustaining air,
It makes the reptile equal to the God . . .
They who inspire it most are fortunate
As I am now; but those who feel it most
Are happier still, after long sufferings
As I shall soon become.

PANTHEA

List! Spirits speak.

VOICE (*in the air, singing*)

Life of Life! thy lips enkindle
    With their love the breath between them
And thy smiles before they dwindle
    Make the cold air fire; then screen them
In those looks where whoso gazes
Faints, entangled in their mazes.

Child of Light! thy limbs are burning
    Through the vest which seems to hide them
As the radiant lines of morning
    Through the clouds ere they divide them,

And this atmosphere divinest
Shrouds thee wheresoe'er thou shinest.

Fair are others—none beholds thee
   But thy voice sounds low and tender
Like the fairest—for it folds thee
   From the sight, that liquid splendor,
And all feel, yet see thee never
As I feel now, lost forever!

Lamp of Earth! where'er thou movest
   Its dim shapes are clad with brightness
And the souls of whom thou lovest
   Walk upon the winds with lightness
Till they fail, as I am failing,
Dizzy, lost . . . yet unbewailing!

ASIA

   My soul is an enchanted Boat
   Which, like a sleeping swan, doth float
Upon the silver waves of thy sweet singing,
   And thine doth like an Angel sit
   Beside the helm conducting it
Whilst all the winds with melody are ringing.
   It seems to float ever—forever—
   Upon that many winding River
   Between mountains, woods, abysses,
   A Paradise of wildernesses,
Till like one in slumber bound
Borne to the Ocean, I float down, around,
Into a Sea profound, of ever-spreading sound.

   Meanwhile thy Spirit lifts its pinions
   In Music's most serene dominions,
Catching the winds that fan that happy Heaven.
   And we sail on, away, afar,

Without a course—without a star—
But by the instinct of sweet Music driven
   Till, through Elysian garden islets
   By thee, most beautiful of pilots,
   Where never mortal pinnace glided,
   The boat of my desire is guided—
Realms where the air we breathe is Love
Which in the winds and on the waves doth move,
Harmonizing this Earth with what we feel above.

   We have passed Age's icy caves,
   And Manhood's dark and tossing waves
And Youth's smooth ocean, smiling to betray;
   Beyond the glassy gulfs we flee
   Of shadow-peopled Infancy,
Through Death and Birth to a diviner day,
   A Paradise of vaulted bowers
   Lit by downward-gazing flowers
   And watery paths that wind between
   Wildernesses calm and green,
Peopled by shapes too bright to see,
And rest, having beheld—somewhat like thee,
Which walk upon the sea, and chaunt melodiously!

From ACT III

Heaven. Jupiter *on his Throne;* Thetis *and the other Deities assembled.*

JUPITER

Ye congregated Powers of Heaven who share
The glory and the strength of him ye serve,
Rejoice! henceforth I am omnipotent.
All else has been subdued to me—alone
The soul of man, like unextinguished fire,
Yet burns towards Heaven with fierce reproach and doubt
And lamentation and reluctant prayer,
Hurling up insurrection, which might make
Our antique empire insecure, though built
On eldest faith, and Hell's coeval, fear.
And though my curses through the pendulous air
Like snow on herbless peaks, fall flake by flake
And cling to it—though under my wrath's night
It climb the crags of life, step after step,
Which wound it, as ice wounds unsandaled feet,
It yet remains supreme o'er misery.
Aspiring . . . unrepressed; yet soon to fall:
Even now have I begotten a strange wonder,
That fatal Child, the terror of the Earth,
Who waits but till the destined Hour arrive,
Bearing from Demogorgon's vacant throne
The dreadful might of everliving limbs
Which clothed that awful spirit unbeheld—
To redescend and trample out the spark . . .

Pour forth Heaven's wine, Idaean Ganymede,
And let it fill the daedal cups like fire

And from the flower-inwoven soil divine
Ye all triumphant harmonies arise
As dew from Earth under the twilight stars;
Drink! be the nectar circling through your veins
The soul of joy, ye everliving Gods,
Till exultation burst in one wide voice
Like music from Elysian winds—
                              And thou
Ascend beside me, veiled in the light
Of the desire which makes thee one with me,
Thetis, bright Image of Eternity!—
When thou didst cry, "Insufferable might!
God! spare me! I sustain not the quick flames,
The penetrating presence; all my being,
Like him whom the Numidian seps did thaw
Into a dew with poison, is dissolved,
Sinking through its foundations"—even then
Two mighty spirits, mingling, made a third
Mightier than either—which unbodied now
Between us, floats, felt although unbeheld,
Waiting the incarnation, which ascends—
Hear ye the thunder of the fiery wheels
Griding the winds?—from Demogorgon's throne—
Victory! victory! Feel'st thou not, O World,
The Earthquake of his chariot thundering up
Olympus?
[*The Car of the* Hour *arrives.* Demogorgon *descends
and moves towards the Throne of* Jupiter.]
                    Awful Shape, what art thou? Speak!

DEMOGORGON

Eternity—demand no direr name.
Descend, and follow me down the abyss;
I am thy child, as thou wert Saturn's child,
Mightier than thee; and we must dwell together
Henceforth in darkness—Lift thy lightnings not.

The tyranny of Heaven none may retain,
Or reassume, or hold succeeding thee . . .
Yet if thou wilt—as 'tis the destiny
Of trodden worms to writhe till they are dead—
Put forth thy might.

JUPITER

                    Detested prodigy!
Even thus beneath the deep Titanian prisons
I trample thee! . . . Thou lingerest?

                                        Mercy! mercy!
No pity—no release, no respite! . . . Oh,
That thou wouldst make mine enemy my judge.
Even where he hangs, seared by my long revenge
On Caucasus—he would not doom me thus—
Gentle and just and dreadless, is he not
The monarch of the world?—what then art thou? . . .
No refuge! no appeal— . . .

                              Sink with me then—
We two will sink in the wide waves of ruin
Even as a vulture and a snake outspent
Drop, twisted in inextricable fight,
Into a shoreless sea—Let Hell unlock
Its mounded Oceans of tempestuous fire,
And whelm on them into the bottomless void
The desolated world and thee and me,
The conqueror and the conquered, and the wreck
Of that for which they combated.

                                    Ai! Ai!
The elements obey me not . . . I sink . . .
Dizzily down—ever, forever, down—
And, like a cloud, mine enemy above
Darkens my fall with victory!—Ai! Ai!

       ✿   ✿   ✿   ✿   ✿   ✿   ✿

SCENE III

Caucasus. Prometheus, Hercules, Ione, *the* Earth, Spirits. Asia *and* Panthea *borne in the Car with the* Spirit of the Hour. Hercules *unbinds* Prometheus, *who descends.*

HERCULES

Most glorious among Spirits, thus doth strength
To wisdom, courage, and long suffering love,
And thee, who art the form they animate,
Minister, like a slave.

PROMETHEUS

          Thy gentle words
Are sweeter even than freedom long desired
And long delayed.
          Asia, thou light of life,
Shadow of beauty unbeheld; and ye
Fair sister nymphs, who made long years of pain
Sweet to remember through your love and care:
Henceforth we will not part. There is a Cave
All overgrown with trailing odorous plants
Which curtain out the day with leaves and flowers
And paved with veined emerald, and a fountain
Leaps in the midst with an awakening sound;
From its curved roof the mountain's frozen tears
Like snow or silver or long diamond spires
Hang downward, raining forth a doubtful light;
And there is heard the ever-moving air
Whispering without from tree to tree, and birds,
And bees; and all around are mossy seats
And the rough walls are clothed with long soft grass;
A simple dwelling, which shall be our own,
Where we will sit and talk of time and change
As the world ebbs and flows, ourselves unchanged—

What can hide man from Mutability?—
And if ye sigh, then I will smile, and thou
Ione, shall chant fragments of sea music,
Until I weep, when ye shall smile away
The tears she brought, which yet were sweet to shed;
We will entangle buds and flowers, and beams
Which twinkle on the fountain's brim, and make
Strange combinations out of common things
Like human babes in their brief innocence;
And we will search, with looks and words of love
For hidden thoughts each lovelier than the last,
Our unexhausted spirits, and like lutes
Touched by the skill of the enamored wind,
Weave harmonies divine, yet ever new,
From difference sweet where discord cannot be.
And hither come, sped on the charmed winds
Which meet from all the points of Heaven, as bees
From every flower aerial Enna feeds
At their known island homes in Himera,
The echoes of the human world, which tell
Of the low voice of love, almost unheard,
And dove-eyed pity's murmured pain and music,
Itself the echo of the heart, and all
That tempers or improves man's life, now free.
And lovely apparitions dim at first
Then radiant—as the mind, arising bright
From the embrace of beauty (whence the forms
Of which these are the phantoms) casts on them
The gathered rays which are reality—
Shall visit us, the progeny immortal
Of Painting, Sculpture and rapt Poesy
And arts, though unimagined, yet to be.
The wandering voices and the shadows these
Of all that man becomes, the mediators
Of that best worship, love, by him and us
Given and returned, swift shapes and sounds which grow

More fair and soft as man grows wise and kind,
And veil by veil evil and error fall . . .
Such virtue has the cave and place around.
                        [*Turning to the* Spirit of the Hour.]
For thee, fair Spirit, one toil remains. Ione,
Give her that curved shell which Proteus old
Made Asia's nuptial boon, breathing within it
A voice to be accomplished, and which thou
Didst hide in grass under the hollow rock.

IONE

Thou most desired Hour, more loved and lovely
Than all thy sisters, this is the mystic shell;
See the pale azure fading into silver,
Lining it with a soft yet glowing light.
Looks it not like lulled music sleeping there?

SPIRIT

It seems in truth the fairest shell of Ocean:
Its sound must be at once both sweet and strange.

PROMETHEUS

Go, borne over the cities of mankind
On whirlwind-footed coursers! once again
Outspeed the sun around the orbed world
And as thy chariot cleaves the kindling air,
Thou breathe into the many-folded Shell,
Loosening its mighty music; it shall be
As thunder mingled with clear echoes—Then
Return and thou shalt dwell beside our cave.
                        [*Kissing the ground.*]
And thou, O Mother Earth!—

THE EARTH

                    I hear—I feel—
Thy lips are on me, and their touch runs down

Even to the adamantine central gloom
Along these marble nerves—'tis life, 'tis joy,
And through my withered, old and icy frame
The warmth of an immortal youth shoots down
Circling—Henceforth the many children fair
Folded in my sustaining arms—all plants,
And creeping forms, and insects rainbow-winged
And birds and beasts and fish and human shapes
Which drew disease and pain from my wan bosom,
Draining the poison of despair—shall take
And interchange sweet nutriment; to me
Shall they become like sister-antelopes
By one fair dam, snowwhite and swift as wind
Nursed among lilies near a brimming stream;
The dewmists of my sunless sleep shall float
Under the stars like balm; night-folded flowers
Shall suck unwithering hues in their repose;
And men and beasts in happy dreams shall gather
Strength for the coming day and all its joy:
And death shall be the last embrace of her
Who takes the life she gave, even as a mother
Folding her child, says, "Leave me not again!"

ASIA

O mother! wherefore speak the name of death?
Cease they to love and move and breathe and speak
Who die?

THE EARTH

It would avail not to reply:
Thou art immortal and this tongue is known
But to the uncommunicating dead—
Death is the veil which those who live call life:
They sleep—and it is lifted . . . and meanwhile
In mild variety the seasons mild

With rainbow-skirted showers, and odorous winds
And long blue meteors cleansing the dull night,
And the life-kindling shafts of the keen Sun's
All-piercing bow, and the dew-mingled rain
Of the calm moonbeams, a soft influence mild;
Shall clothe the forests and the fields—aye, even
The crag-built deserts of the barren deep—
With ever-living leaves and fruits and flowers.
And Thou! There is a Cavern where my spirit
Was panted forth in anguish whilst thy pain
Made my heart mad, and those who did inhale it
Became mad too, and built a Temple there
And spoke and were oracular, and lured
The erring nations round to mutual war
And faithless faith, such as Jove kept with thee;
Which breath now rises as among tall weeds
A violet's exhalation, and it fills
With a serener light and crimson air
Intense yet soft the rocks and woods around;
It feeds the quick growth of the Serpent vine
And the dark linked ivy tangling wild
And budding, blown, or odor-faded blooms
Which star the winds with points of colored light
As they rain through them, and bright, golden globes
Of fruit, suspended in their own green heaven;
And, through their veined leaves and amber stems,
The flowers whose purple and translucid bowls
Stand ever mantling with aerial dew,
The drink of spirits; and it circles round
Like the soft waving wings of noonday dreams,
Inspiring calm and happy thoughts, like mine
Now thou art thus restored . . . This Cave is thine.
Arise! Appear!

     ❀   ❀   ❀   ❀   ❀   ❀   ❀

A Forest. In the Background a Cave. Prometheus,
Asia, Panthea, Ione, *and the* Spirit of the Earth.

PANTHEA

It is the delicate spirit
That guides the earth through Heaven. From afar
The populous constellations call that light
The loveliest of the planets, and sometimes
It floats along the spray of the salt sea
Or makes its chariot of a foggy cloud
Or walks through fields or cities while men sleep
Or o'er the mountaintops, or down the rivers,
Or through the green waste wilderness, as now,
Wondering at all it sees. Before Jove reigned
It loved our sister Asia, and it came
Each leisure hour to drink the liquid light
Out of her eyes, for which it said it thirsted
As one bit by a dipsas; and with her
It made its childish confidence, and told her
All it had known or seen, for it saw much,
Yet idly reasoned what it saw; and called her—
For whence it sprung it knew not nor do I—
"Mother, dear Mother."

    ❊   ❊   ❊   ❊   ❊   ❊   ❊

PROMETHEUS

We feel what thou hast heard and seen—yet speak.

SPIRIT OF THE HOUR

Soon as the sound had ceased whose thunder filled
The abysses of the sky, and the wide earth,
There was a change . . . the impalpable thin air
And the all-circling sunlight were transformed

As if the sense of love dissolved in them
Had folded itself round the sphered world.
My vision then grew clear and I could see
Into the mysteries of the Universe.
Dizzy as with delight I floated down,
Winnowing the lightsome air with languid plumes,
My coursers sought their birthplace in the sun
Where they henceforth will live exempt from toil,
Pasturing flowers of vegetable fire—
And where my moonlike car will stand within
A temple, gazed upon by Phidian forms,
Of thee, and Asia and the Earth, and me
And you fair nymphs, looking the love we feel,
In memory of the tidings it has borne,
Beneath a dome fretted with graven flowers,
Poised on twelve columns of resplendent stone
And open to the bright and liquid sky.
Yoked to it by an amphisbaenic snake
The likeness of those winged steeds will mock
The flight from which they find repose—Alas,
Whither has wandered now my partial tongue
When all remains untold which ye would hear!—
As I have said, I floated to the Earth:
It was, as it is still, the pain of bliss
To move, to breathe, to be; I wandering went
Among the haunts and dwellings of mankind
And first was disappointed not to see
Such mighty change as I had felt within
Expressed in outward things; but soon I looked,
And behold! thrones were kingless, and men walked
One with the other even as spirits do,
None fawned, none trampled; hate, disdain or fear,
Self-love or self-contempt on human brows
No more inscribed, as o'er the gate of hell,
"All hope abandon, ye who enter here";
None frowned, none trembled, none with eager fear

Gazed on another's eye of cold command
Until the subject of a tyrant's will
Became, worse fate, the abject of his own
Which spurred him, like an outspent horse, to death.
None wrought his lips in truth-entangling lines
Which smiled the lie his tongue disdained to speak;
None with firm sneer trod out in his own heart
The sparks of love and hope, till there remained
Those bitter ashes, a soul self-consumed,
And the wretch crept, a vampire among men,
Infecting all with his own hideous ill.
None talked that common, false, cold, hollow talk
Which makes the heart deny the *yes* it breathes
Yet question that unmeant hypocrisy
With such a self-mistrust as has no name.
And women too, frank, beautiful and kind
As the free Heaven which rains fresh light and dew
On the wide earth, past: gentle, radiant forms,
From custom's evil taint exempt and pure;
Speaking the wisdom once they could not think,
Looking emotions once they feared to feel
And changed to all which once they dared not be,
Yet being now, made Earth like Heaven—nor pride
Nor jealousy nor envy nor ill shame,
The bitterest of those drops of treasured gall,
Spoilt the sweet taste of the nepenthe, love.

Thrones, altars, judgment seats and prisons; wherein
And beside which, by wretched men were borne
Scepters, tiaras, swords and chains, and tomes
Of reasoned wrong glozed on by ignorance,
Were like those monstrous and barbaric shapes,
The ghosts of a no more remembered fame,
Which from their unworn obelisks look forth
In triumph o'er the palaces and tombs
Of those who were their conquerors, moldering round.

Those imaged to the pride of Kings and Priests
A dark yet mighty faith, a power as wide
As is the world it wasted, and are now
But an astonishment; even so the tools
And emblems of its last captivity
Amid the dwellings of the peopled Earth,
Stand, not o'erthrown, but unregarded now.
And those foul shapes, abhorred by God and man—
Which under many a name and many a form
Strange, savage, ghastly, dark and execrable
Were Jupiter, the tyrant of the world;
And which the nations panic-stricken served
With blood, and hearts broken by long hope, and love
Dragged to his altars soiled and garlandless
And slain amid men's unreclaiming tears,
Flattering the thing they feared, which fear was hate—
Frown, moldering fast, o'er their abandoned shrines.
The painted veil, by those who were, called life,
Which mimicked, as with colors idly spread,
All men believed and hoped, is torn aside—
The loathsome mask has fallen, the man remains
Scepterless, free, uncircumscribed—but man:
Equal, unclassed, tribeless and nationless,
Exempt from awe, worship, degree—the King
Over himself; just, gentle, wise—but man:
Passionless? no—yet free from guilt or pain
Which were, for his will made, or suffered them,
Nor yet exempt, though ruling them like slaves,
From chance and death and mutability,
The clogs of that which else might oversoar
The loftiest star of unascended Heaven
Pinnacled dim in the intense inane.

From ACT IV

Scene: A Part of the Forest near the Cave of Prometheus. Panthea *and* Ione *are sleeping: they awaken gradually during the first Song.*

IONE

           Even whilst we speak
New notes arise . . . What is that awful sound?

PANTHEA

'Tis the deep music of the rolling world,
Kindling within the strings of the waved air
Aeolian modulations.

IONE

           Listen too,
How every pause is filled with undernotes,
Clear, silver, icy, keen, awakening tones
Which pierce the sense and live within the soul
As the sharp stars pierce Winter's crystal air
And gaze upon themselves within the sea.

PANTHEA

But see, where through two openings in the forest
Which hanging branches overcanopy,
And where two runnels of a rivulet
Between the close moss violet-inwoven
Have made their path of melody, like sisters
Who part with sighs that they may meet in smiles,
Turning their dear disunion to an isle
Of lovely grief, a wood of sweet sad thoughts;
Two visions of strange radiance float upon
The Oceanlike enchantment of strong sound

Which flows intenser, keener, deeper yet
Under the ground and through the windless air.

IONE

I see a chariot like that thinnest boat
In which the Mother of the Months is borne
By ebbing light into her western cave
When she upsprings from interlunar dreams,
O'er which is curved an orblike canopy
Of gentle darkness, and the hills and woods
Distinctly seen through that dusk aery veil
Regard like shapes in an enchanter's glass;
Its wheels are solid clouds, azure and gold,
Such as the genii of the thunderstorm
Pile on the floor of the illumined sea
When the Sun rushes under it; they roll
And move and grow as with an inward wind.
Within it sits a winged Infant, white
Its countenance, like the whiteness of bright snow,
Its plumes are as feathers of sunny frost,
Its limbs gleam white, through the wind-flowing folds
Of its white robe, woof of ethereal pearl.
Its hair is white—the brightness of white light
Scattered in strings, yet its two eyes are Heavens
Of liquid darkness, which the Deity
Within, seems pouring, as a storm is poured
From jagged clouds, out of their arrowy lashes,
Tempering the cold and radiant air around
With fire that is not brightness; in its hand
It sways a quivering moonbeam, from whose point
A guiding power directs the chariot's prow
Over its wheeled clouds, which as they roll
Over the grass and flowers and waves, wake sounds
Sweet as a singing rain of silver dew.

And from the other opening in the wood
Rushes with loud and whirlwind harmony
A sphere, which is as many thousand spheres,
Solid as crystal, yet through all its mass
Flow, as through empty space, music and light:
Ten thousand orbs involving and involved,
Purple and azure, white and green and golden,
Sphere within sphere, and every space between
Peopled with unimaginable shapes
Such as ghosts dream dwell in the lampless deep
Yet each intertranspicuous, and they whirl
Over each other with a thousand motions
Upon a thousand sightless axles spinning
And with the force of self-destroying swiftness,
Intensely, slowly, solemnly roll on—
Kindling with mingled sounds, and many tones,
Intelligible words and music wild—
With mighty whirl the multidinous Orb
Grinds the bright brook into an azure mist
Of elemental subtlety, like light,
And the wild odor of the forest flowers,
The music of the living grass and air,
The emerald light of leaf-entangled beams
Round its intense, yet self-conflicting speed,
Seem kneaded into one aerial mass
Which drowns the sense. Within the Orb itself,
Pillowed upon its alabaster arms
Like to a child o'erwearied with sweet toil,
On its own folded wings and wavy hair
The Spirit of the Earth is laid asleep,
And you can see its little lips are moving
Amid the changing light of their own smiles
Like one who talks of what he loves in dream—

IONE

'Tis only mocking the Orb's harmony . . .

PANTHEA

And from a star upon its forehead, shoot,
Like swords of azure fire, or golden spears
With tyrant-quelling myrtle overtwined,
Embleming Heaven and Earth united now,
Vast beams like spokes of some invisible wheel
Which whirl as the Orb whirls, swifter than thought,
Filling the abyss with sunlike lightenings,
And perpendicular now, and now transverse,
Pierce the dark soil, and as they pierce and pass
Make bare the secrets of the Earth's deep heart,
Infinite mine of adamant and gold,
Valueless stones and unimagined gems,
And caverns on crystalline columns poised
With vegetable silver overspread,
Wells of unfathomed fire, and watersprings
Whence the great Sea, even as a child, is fed
Whose vapors clothe Earth's monarch mountaintops
With kingly, ermine snow; the beams flash on
And make appear the melancholy ruins
Of canceled cycles; anchors, beaks of ships,
Planks turned to marble, quivers, helms and spears
And gorgon-headed targes, and the wheels
Of scythed chariots, and the emblazonry
Of trophies, standards and armorial beasts
Round which Death laughed, sepulchered emblems
Of dead Destruction, ruin within ruin!
The wrecks beside of many a city vast,
Whose population which the Earth grew over
Was mortal but not human; see, they lie,
Their monstrous works and uncouth skeletons,
Their statues, homes, and fanes; prodigious shapes
Huddled in gray annihilation, split,

Jammed in the hard black deep; and over these
The anatomies of unknown winged things,
And fishes which were isles of living scale,
And serpents, bony chains, twisted around
The iron crags, or within heaps of dust
To which the tortuous strength of their last pangs
Had crushed the iron crags—and over these
The jagged alligator and the might
Of earth-convulsing behemoth, which once
Were monarch beasts, and on the slimy shores
And weed-overgrown continents of Earth
Increased and multiplied like summer worms
On an abandoned corpse, till the blue globe
Wrapped Deluge round it like a cloak, and they
Yelled, gasped and were abolished; or some God
Whose throne was in a Comet, past, and cried—
"Be not!"—and like my words they were no more.

The Earth

The joy, the triumph, the delight, the madness,
The boundless, overflowing bursting gladness,
The vaporous exultation, not to be confined!
   Ha! ha! the animation of delight
   Which wraps me, like an atmosphere of light,
And bears me as a cloud is borne by its own wind!

The Moon

   Brother mine, calm wanderer,
    Happy globe of land and air,
Some Spirit is darted like a beam from thee,
    Which penetrates my frozen frame
    And passes with the warmth of flame—
With love and odor and deep melody
    Through me, through me!—

THE EARTH

Ha! ha! the caverns of my hollow mountains,
My cloven fire-crags, sound-exulting fountains
Laugh with a vast and inextinguishable laughter.
   The Oceans and the Deserts and the Abysses
   And the deep air's unmeasured wildernesses
Answer from all their clouds and billows, echoing after.

   They cry aloud as I do—"Sceptered Curse,
   Who all our green and azure Universe
Threatenedst to muffle round with black destruction, sending
   A solid cloud to rain hot thunderstones,
   And splinter and knead down my children's bones,
All I bring forth, to one void mass battering and blending,

   "Until each craglike tower and storied column,
   Palace and Obelisk and Temple solemn,
My imperial mountains crowned with cloud and snow
     and fire,
   My sealike forests, every blade and blossom
   Which finds a grave or cradle in my bosom,
Were stamped by thy strong hate into a lifeless mire,
   "How art thou sunk, withdrawn, cover'd—drunk up
   By thirsty nothing, as the brackish cup
Drained by a Desert-troop—a little drop for all;
   And from beneath, around, within, above,
   Filling thy void annihilation, Love
Bursts in like light on caves cloven by the thunderball."

THE MOON

The snow upon my lifeless mountains
Is loosened into living fountains,
My solid Oceans flow and sing and shine
   A spirit from my heart bursts forth,

It clothes with unexpected birth
My cold bare bosom: Oh! it must be thine
    On mine, on mine!

Gazing on thee I feel, I know,
    Green stalks burst forth, and bright flowers grow
And living shapes upon my bosom move:
    Music is in the sea and air,
    Winged clouds soar here and there,
Dark with the rain new buds are dreaming of:
        'Tis Love, all Love!

THE EARTH

It interpenetrates my granite mass,
    Through tangled roots and trodden clay doth pass
Into the utmost leaves and delicatest flowers;
    Upon the winds, among the clouds 'tis spread,
    It wakes a life in the forgotten dead,
They breathe a spirit up from their obscurest bowers

And like a storm, bursting its cloudy prison
    With thunder and with whirlwind, has arisen
Out of the lampless caves of unimagined being,
    With earthquake shock and swiftness making shiver
    Thought's stagnant chaos, unremoved forever,
Till Hate and Fear and Pain, light-vanquished shadows,
    fleeing

Leave Man, who was a many-sided mirror
    Which could distort to many a shape of error
This true fair world of things—a Sea reflecting Love;
    Which over all his kind, as the Sun's Heaven
    Gliding o'er Ocean, smooth, serene and even,
Darting from starry depths radiance and light, doth move,
    Leave Man, even as a leprous child is left
    Who follows a sick beast to some warm cleft

Of rocks, through which the might of healing springs is poured;
    Then when it wanders home with rosy smile
    Unconscious, and its mother fears awhile
It is a Spirit—then weeps on her child restored.

    Man, oh, not men! a chain of linked thought,
    Of love and might to be divided not,
Compelling the elements with adamantine stress—
    As the Sun rules, even with a tyrant's gaze,
    The unquiet Republic of the maze
Of planets, struggling fierce towards Heaven's free wilderness.

    Man, one harmonious Soul of many a soul
    Whose nature is its own divine control
Where all things flow to all, as rivers to the sea;
    Familiar acts are beautiful through love;
    Labor and Pain and Grief in life's green grove
Sport like tame beasts—none knew how gentle they could be!

    His Will, with all mean passions, bad delights,
    And selfish cares, its trembling satellites,
A spirit ill to guide, but mighty to obey,
    Is as a tempest-winged ship, whose helm
    Love rules, through waves which dare not overwhelm,
Forcing life's wildest shores to own its sovereign sway.

    All things confess his strength—Through the cold mass
    Of marble and of color his dreams pass;
Bright threads, whence mothers weave the robes their children
        wear;
    Language is a perpetual Orphic song,
    Which rules with Daedal harmony a throng
Of thoughts and forms, which else senseless and shapeless were.

    The Lightning is his slave; Heaven's utmost deep
    Gives up her stars, and like a flock of sheep

They pass before his eye, are numbered, and roll on!
　　The Tempest is his steed—he strides the air;
　　And the abyss shouts from her depth laid bare,
"Heaven, hast thou secrets? Man unveils me, I have none."

THE MOON

　　The shadow of white Death has past
　　From my path in Heaven at last,
A clinging shroud of solid frost and sleep—
　　And through my newly-woven bowers
　　Wander happy paramours
Less mighty, but as mild as those who keep
　　　　Thy vales more deep.

THE EARTH

　　As the dissolving warmth of Dawn may fold
　　A half-unfrozen dewglobe, green and gold
And crystalline, till it becomes a winged mist
　　And wanders up the vault of the blue Day,
　　Outlives the noon, and on the Sun's last ray
Hangs o'er the Sea—a fleece of fire and amethyst—

THE MOON

　　Thou art folded, thou art lying
　　In the light which is undying
Of thine own joy and Heaven's smile divine;
　　All suns and constellations shower
　　On thee a light, a life, a power
Which doth array thy sphere—thou pourest thine
　　　　On mine, on mine!

THE EARTH

　　I spin beneath my pyramid of night
　　Which points into the Heavens, dreaming delight,
Murmuring victorious joy in my enchanted sleep;

As a youth lulled in love-dreams, faintly sighing,
  Under the shadow of his beauty lying
Which round his rest a watch of light and warmth doth keep.

THE MOON

  As in the soft and sweet eclipse
  When soul meets soul on lovers' lips,
High hearts are calm and brightest eyes are dull;
  So when thy shadow falls on me
  Then am I mute and still—by thee
Covered; of thy love, Orb most beautiful,
    Full, oh, too full!—

  Thou art speeding round the Sun,
  Brightest World of many a one,
  Green and azure sphere, which shinest
  With a light which is divinest
  Among all the lamps of Heaven
  To whom life and light is given;
  I, thy crystal paramour,
  Borne beside thee by a power
  Like the polar Paradise,
  Magnet-like, of lovers' eyes;
  I, a most enamored maiden
  Whose weak brain is overladen
  With the pleasure of her love—
  Maniac-like around thee move,
  Gazing, an insatiate bride,
  On thy form from every side
  Like a Maenad round the cup
  Which Agave lifted up
  In the weird Cadmaean forest—
  Brother, wheresoe'er thou soarest
  I must hurry, whirl and follow
  Through the Heavens wide and hollow,
  Sheltered by the warm embrace

Of thy soul, from hungry space,
Drinking, from thy sense and sight
Beauty, majesty, and might,
As a lover or chameleon
Grows like what it looks upon,
As a violet's gentle eye
Gazes on the azure sky
Until its hue grows like what it beholds,
As a gray and watery mist
Glows like solid amethyst
Athwart the western mountains it enfolds,
When the sunset sleeps
Upon its snow—

THE EARTH

And the weak day weeps
That it should be so.
O gentle Moon, the voice of thy delight
Falls on me like thy clear and tender light
Soothing the seaman, borne the summer night
Through isles forever calm;
O gentle Moon, thy crystal accents pierce
The caverns of my Pride's deep Universe,
Charming the tiger Joy, whose tramplings fierce
Made wounds, which need thy balm.

✿   ✿   ✿   ✿   ✿   ✿   ✿

DEMOGORGON

Man, who wert once a despot and a slave—
A dupe and a deceiver—a Decay,
A Traveler from the cradle to the grave
Through the dim night of this immortal Day:

ALL

Speak—thy strong words may never pass away.

DEMOGORGON

This is the Day which down the void Abysm
At the Earth-born's spell yawns for Heaven's Despotism,
   And Conquest is dragged Captive through the Deep;
Love from its awful throne of patient power
In the wise heart, from the last giddy hour
   Of dread endurance, from the slippery, steep,
And narrow verge of crag-like Agony, springs
And folds over the world its healing wings.

Gentleness, Virtue, Wisdom and Endurance—
These are the seals of that most firm assurance
   Which bars the pit over Destruction's strength;
And if, with infirm hand, Eternity,
Mother of many acts and hours, should free
   The serpent that would clasp her with his length—
These are the spells by which to reassume
An empire o'er the disentangled Doom.

To suffer woes which Hope thinks infinite;
To forgive wrongs darker than Death or Night;
   To defy Power which seems Omnipotent;
To love, and bear; to hope, till Hope creates
From its own wreck the thing it contemplates;
   Neither to change nor falter nor repent:
This, like thy glory, Titan! is to be
Good, great and joyous, beautiful and free;
This is alone Life, Joy, Empire and Victory.

Epipsychidion

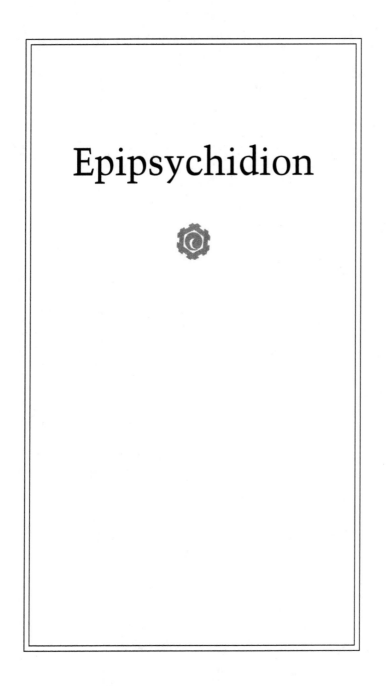

EPIPSYCHIDION

Sweet Spirit! Sister of that orphan one,
Whose empire is the name thou weepest on,
In my heart's temple I suspend to thee
These votive wreaths of withered memory.

Poor captive bird! who, from thy narrow cage,
Pourest such music, that it might assuage
The rugged hearts of those who prisoned thee,
Were they not deaf to all sweet melody;
This song shall be thy rose: its petals pale
Are dead, indeed, my adored Nightingale!
But soft and fragrant is the faded blossom,
And it has no thorn left to wound thy bosom.

High, spirit-winged Heart! who dost forever
Beat thine unfeeling bars with vain endeavor,
Till those bright plumes of thought, in which arrayed
It oversoared this low and worldly shade,
Lie shattered; and thy panting, wounded breast
Stains with dear blood its unmaternal nest!
I weep vain tears: blood would less bitter be,
Yet poured forth gladlier, could it profit thee.

Seraph of Heaven! too gentle to be human,
Veiling beneath that radiant form of Woman
All that is insupportable in thee
Of light, and love, and immortality!
Sweet Benediction in the eternal Curse!
Veiled Glory of this lampless Universe!
Thou Moon beyond the clouds! Thou living Form
Among the Dead! Thou Star above the Storm!

Thou Wonder, and thou Beauty, and thou Terror!
Thou Harmony of Nature's art! Thou Mirror
In whom, as in the splendor of the Sun,
All shapes look glorious which thou gazest on!
Aye, even the dim words which obscure thee now
Flash, lightning-like, with unaccustomed glow;
I pray thee that thou blot from this sad song
All of its much mortality and wrong,
With those clear drops, which start like sacred dew
From the twin lights thy sweet soul darkens through,
Weeping, till sorrow becomes ecstasy:
Then smile on it, so that it may not die.

I never thought before my death to see
Youth's vision thus made perfect. Emily,
I love thee; though the world by no thin name
Will hide that love from its unvalued shame.
Would we two had been twins of the same mother!
Or, that the name my heart lent to another
Could be a sister's bond for her and thee,
Blending two beams of one eternity!
Yet were one lawful and the other true,
These names, though dear, could paint not, as is due,
How beyond refuge I am thine. Ah me!
I am not thine: I am a part of *thee*.

Sweet Lamp! my mothlike Muse has burnt its wings;
Or, like a dying swan who soars and sings,
Young Love should teach Time, in his own gray style,
All that thou art. Art thou not void of guile,
A lovely soul formed to be blest and bless?
A well of sealed and secret happiness,
Whose waters like blithe light and music are,
Vanquishing dissonance and gloom? A Star
Which moves not in the moving Heavens, alone?
A smile amid dark frowns? a gentle tone

Amid rude voices? a beloved light?
A Solitude, a Refuge, a Delight?
A lute, which those whom love has taught to play
Make music on, to soothe the roughest day
And lull fond grief asleep? a buried treasure?
A cradle of young thoughts of wingless pleasure?
A violet-shrouded grave of Woe?—I measure
The world of fancies, seeking one like thee,
And find—alas! mine own infirmity.

She met me, Stranger, upon life's rough way,
And lured me towards sweet Death; as Night by Day,
Winter by Spring, or Sorrow by swift Hope,
Led into light, life, peace. An antelope,
In the suspended impulse of its lightness,
Were less ethereally light: the brightness
Of her divinest presence trembles through
Her limbs, as underneath a cloud of dew
Embodied in the windless Heaven of June
Amid the splendor-winged stars, the Moon
Burns, inextinguishably beautiful:
And from her lips, as from a hyacinth full
Of honeydew, a liquid murmur drops,
Killing the sense with passion; sweet as stops
Of planetary music heard in trance.
In her mild lights the starry spirits dance,
The sunbeams of those wells which ever leap
Under the lightnings of the soul—too deep
For the brief fathom line of thought or sense.
The glory of her being, issuing thence,
Stains the dead, blank, cold air with a warm shade
Of unentangled intermixture, made
By Love, of light and motion: one intense
Diffusion, one serene Omnipresence,
Whose flowing outlines mingle in their flowing,
Around her cheeks and utmost fingers glowing

With the unintermitted blood, which there
Quivers, (as in a fleece of snowlike air
The crimson pulse of living morning quiver,)
Continuously prolonged, and ending never,
Till they are lost, and in that Beauty furled
Which penetrates and clasps and fills the world;
Scarce visible from extreme loveliness.
Warm fragrance seems to fall from her light dress,
And her loose hair; and where some heavy tress
The air of her own speed has disentwined,
The sweetness seems to satiate the faint wind;
And in the soul a wild odor is felt,
Beyond the sense, like fiery dews that melt
Into the bosom of a frozen bud—
See where she stands! a mortal shape indued
With love and life and light and deity,
And motion which may change but cannot die;
An image of some bright Eternity;
A shadow of some golden dream; a Splendor
Leaving the third sphere pilotless; a tender
Reflection of the eternal Moon of Love
Under whose motions life's dull billows move;
A Metaphor of Spring and Youth and Morning;
A Vision like incarnate April, warning,
With smiles and tears, Frost the Anatomy
Into his summer grave.

                Ah, woe is me!
What have I dared? where am I lifted? how
Shall I descend, and perish not? I know
That Love makes all things equal: I have heard
By mine own heart this joyous truth averred:
The spirit of the worm beneath the sod
In love and worship, blends itself with God.

    Spouse! Sister! Angel! Pilot of the Fate
Whose course has been so starless! O too late

Beloved! O too soon adored, by me!
For in the fields of immortality
My spirit should at first have worshipped thine,
A divine presence in a place divine;
Or should have moved beside it on this earth,
A shadow of that substance, from its birth;
But not as now—I love thee; yes, I feel
That on the fountain of my heart a seal
Is set, to keep its waters pure and bright
For thee, since in those *tears* thou hast delight.
We—are we not formed, as notes of music are,
For one another, though dissimilar;
Such difference without discord, as can make
Those sweetest sounds, in which all spirits shake
As trembling leaves in a continuous air?

    Thy wisdom speaks in me, and bids me dare
Beacon the rocks on which high hearts are wrecked.
I never was attached to that great sect,
Whose doctrine is, that each one should select
Out of the crowd a mistress or a friend,
And all the rest, though fair and wise, commend
To cold oblivion, though it is in the code
Of modern morals, and the beaten road
Which those poor slaves with weary footsteps tread,
Who travel to their home among the dead
By the broad highway of the world, and so
With one chained friend, perhaps a jealous foe,
The dreariest and the longest journey go.

    True Love in this differs from gold and clay,
That to divide is not to take away.
Love is like understanding, that grows bright,
Gazing on many truths; 'tis like thy light,
Imagination! which from earth and sky,
And from the depths of human fantasy,

As from a thousand prisms and mirrors, fills
The Universe with glorious beams, and kills
Error, the worm, with many a sunlike arrow
Of its reverberated lightning. Narrow
The heart that loves, the brain that contemplates,
The life that wears, the spirit that creates
One object, and one form, and builds thereby
A sepulcher for its eternity.

Mind from its object differs most in this:
Evil from good; misery from happiness;
The baser from the nobler; the impure
And frail, from what is clear and must endure.
If you divide suffering and dross, you may
Diminish till it is consumed away;
If you divide pleasure and love and thought,
Each part exceeds the whole; and we know not
How much, while any yet remains unshared,
Of pleasure may be gained, of sorrow spared:
This truth is that deep well, whence sages draw
The unenvied light of hope; the eternal law
By which those live, to whom this world of life
Is as a garden ravaged, and whose strife
Tills for the promise of a later birth
The wilderness of this Elysian earth.

There was a Being whom my spirit oft
Met on its visioned wanderings, far aloft,
In the clear golden prime of my youth's dawn,
Upon the fairy isles of sunny lawn,
Amid the enchanted mountains, and the caves
Of divine sleep, and on the airlike waves
Of wonder-level dream, whose tremulous floor
Paved her light steps—on an imagined shore,
Under the gray beak of some promontory
She met me, robed in such exceeding glory,

That I beheld her not. In solitudes
Her voice came to me through the whispering woods,
And from the fountains, and the odors deep
Of flowers, which, like lips murmuring in their sleep
Of the sweet kisses which had lulled them there,
Breathed but of *her* to the enamored air;
And from the breezes whether low or loud,
And from the rain of every passing cloud,
And from the singing of the summer birds,
And from all sounds, all silence. In the words
Of antique verse and high romance—in form,
Sound, color—in whatever checks that Storm
Which with the shattered present chokes the past;
And in that best philosophy, whose taste
Makes this cold common hell, our life, a doom
As glorious as a fiery martyrdom;
Her Spirit was the harmony of truth—

    Then, from the caverns of my dreamy youth
I sprang, as one sandaled with plumes of fire,
And towards the loadstar of my one desire,
I flitted, like a dizzy moth, whose flight
Is as a dead leaf's in the owlet light,
When it would seek in Hesper's setting sphere
A radiant death, a fiery sepulcher,
As if it were a lamp of earthly flame—
But She, whom prayers or tears then could not tame,
Past, like a God throned on a winged planet,
Whose burning plumes to tenfold swiftness fan it,
Into the dreary cone of our life's shade;
And as a man with mighty loss dismayed,
I would have followed, though the grave between
Yawned like a gulf whose specters are unseen:
When a voice said: "O thou of hearts the weakest,
The phantom is beside thee whom thou seekest."
Then!—"where?"—the world's echo answered "where!"

And in that silence, and in my despair,
I questioned every tongueless wind that flew
Over my tower of mourning, if it knew
Whither 'twas fled, this soul out of my soul;
And murmured names and spells which have control
Over the sightless tyrants of our fate;
But neither prayer nor verse could dissipate
The night which closed on her; nor uncreate
That world within this Chaos, mine and me,
Of which she was the veiled Divinity,
The world I say of thoughts that worshipped her:
And therefore I went forth, with hope and fear
And every gentle passion sick to death,
Feeding my course with expectation's breath,
Into the wintry forest of our life;
And struggling through its error with vain strife,
And stumbling in my weakness and my haste,
And half bewildered by new forms, I past,
Seeking among those untaught foresters
If I could find one form resembling hers,
In which she might have masked herself from me.
There—One, whose voice was venomed melody
Sate by a well, under blue nightshade bowers;
The breath of her false mouth was like faint flowers,
Her touch was as electric poison—flame
Out of her looks into my vitals came,
And from her living cheeks and bosom flew
A killing air, which pierced like honeydew
Into the core of my green heart, and lay
Upon its leaves; until, as hair grown gray
O'er a young brow, they hid its unblown prime
With ruins of unseasonable time.

In many mortal forms I rashly sought
The shadow of that idol of my thought?
And some were fair—but beauty dies away:

Others were wise—but honeyed words betray:
And One was true—oh! why not true to me?
Then, as a hunted deer that could not flee,
I turned upon my thoughts, and stood at bay,
Wounded and weak and panting; the cold day
Trembled, for pity of my strife and pain.
When, like a noonday dawn, there shone again
Deliverance. One stood on my path who seemed
As like the glorious shape which I had dreamed,
As is the Moon, whose changes ever run
Into themselves, to the eternal Sun;
The cold chaste Moon, the Queen of Heaven's bright
    isles,
Who makes all beautiful on which she smiles,
That wandering shrine of soft yet icy flame
Which ever is transformed, yet still the same,
And warms not but illumines. Young and fair
As the descended Spirit of that sphere,
She hid me, as the Moon may hide the night
From its own darkness, until all was bright
Between the Heaven and Earth of my calm mind,
And, as a cloud charioted by the wind,
She led me to a cave in that wild place,
And sate beside me, with her downward face
Illumining my slumbers, like the Moon
Waxing and waning o'er Endymion.
And I was laid asleep, spirit and limb,
And all my being became bright or dim
As the Moon's image in a summer sea,
According as she smiled or frowned on me;
And there I lay, within a chaste cold bed:
Alas, I then was nor alive nor dead—
For at her silver voice came Death and Life,
Unmindful each of their accustomed strife,
Masked like twin babes, a sister and a brother,
The wandering hopes of one abandoned mother,

And through the cavern without wings they flew,
And cried "Away, he is not of our crew."
I wept, and though it be a dream, I weep.

What storms then shook the ocean of my sleep,
Blotting that Moon, whose pale and waning lips
Then shrank as in the sickness of eclipse—
And how my soul was as a lampless sea,
And who was then its Tempest; and when She,
The Planet of that hour, was quenched, what frost
Crept o'er those waters, till from coast to coast
The moving billows of my being fell
Into a death of ice, immoveable—
And then—what earthquakes made it gape and split,
The white Moon smiling all the while on it,
These words conceal—If not, each word would be
The key of staunchless tears. Weep not for me!

At length, into the obscure Forest came
The Vision I had sought through grief and shame.
Athwart that wintry wilderness of thorns
Flashed from her motion splendor like the Morn's,
And from her presence life was radiated
Through the gray earth and branches bare and dead;
So that her way was paved, and roofed above
With flowers as soft as thoughts of budding love;
And music from her respiration spread
Like light—all other sounds were penetrated
By the small, still, sweet spirit of that sound,
So that the savage winds hung mute around;
And odors warm and fresh fell from her hair
Dissolving the dull cold in the froze air:
Soft as an Incarnation of the Sun,
When light is changed to love, this glorious One
Floated into the cavern where I lay,
And called my Spirit, and the dreaming clay

Was lifted by the thing that dreamed below
As smoke by fire, and in her beauty's glow
I stood, and felt the dawn of my long night
Was penetrating me with living light:
I knew it was the Vision veiled from me
So many years—that it was Emily.

Twin Spheres of light who rule this passive Earth,
This world of love, this *me*; and into birth
Awaken all its fruits and flowers, and dart
Magnetic might into its central heart;
And lift its billows and its mists, and guide
By everlasting laws, each wind and tide
To its fit cloud, and its appointed cave;
And lull its storms, each in the craggy grave
Which was its cradle, luring to faint bowers
The armies of the rainbow-winged showers;
And, as those married lights, which from the towers
Of Heaven look forth and fold the wandering globe
In liquid sleep and splendor, as a robe;
And all their many mingled influence blend,
If equal, yet unlike, to one sweet end—
So ye, bright regents, with alternate sway
Govern my sphere of being, night and day!
Thou, not disdaining even a borrowed might;
Thou, not eclipsing a remoter light;
And, through the shadow of the seasons three,
From Spring to Autumn's sere maturity,
Light it into the Winter of the tomb,
Where it may ripen to a brighter bloom.
Thou too, O Comet beautiful and fierce,
Who drew the heart of this frail Universe
Towards thine own; till, wrecked in that convulsion,
Alternating attraction and repulsion,
Thine went astray and that was rent in twain;
Oh, float into our azure heaven again!

Be there love's folding star at thy return;
The living Sun will feed thee from its urn
Of golden fire; the Moon will veil her horn
In thy last smiles; adoring Even and Morn
Will worship thee with incense of calm breath
And lights and shadows; as the star of Death
And Birth is worshipped by those sisters wild
Called Hope and Fear—upon the heart are piled
Their offerings—of this sacrifice divine
A World shall be the altar.

                      Lady mine,
Scorn not these flowers of thought, the fading birth
Which from its heart of hearts that plant puts forth
Whose fruit, made perfect by thy sunny eyes,
Will be as of the trees of Paradise.

    The day is come, and thou wilt fly with me.
To whatsoe'er of dull mortality
Is mine, remain a vestal sister still;
To the intense, the deep, the imperishable,
Not mine but me, henceforth be thou united
Even as a bride, delighting and delighted.
The hour is come—the destined Star has risen
Which shall descend upon a vacant prison.
The walls are high, the gates are strong, thick set
The sentinels—but true love never yet
Was thus constrained: it overleaps all fence:
Like lightning, with invisible violence
Piercing its continents; like Heaven's free breath,
Which he who grasps can hold not; liker Death,
Who rides upon a thought, and makes his way
Through temple, tower, and palace, and the array
Of arms: more strength has Love than he or they;
For it can burst his charnel, and make free
The limbs in chains, the heart in agony,
The soul in dust and chaos.

Emily,
A ship is floating in the harbor now,
A wind is hovering o'er the mountain's brow;
There is a path on the sea's azure floor,
No keel has ever plowed that path before;
The halcyons brood around the foamless isles;
The treacherous Ocean has forsworn its wiles;
The merry mariners are bold and free:
Say, my heart's sister, wilt thou sail with me?
Our bark is as an albatross, whose nest
Is a far Eden of the purple East;
And we between her wings will sit, while Night
And Day, and Storm, and Calm, pursue their flight,
Our ministers, along the boundless Sea,
Treading each other's heels, unheededly.
It is an isle under Ionian skies,
Beautiful as a wreck of Paradise,
And, for the harbors are not safe and good,
This land would have remained a solitude
But for some pastoral people native there,
Who from the Elysian, clear, and golden air
Draw the last spirit of the age of gold,
Simple and spirited; innocent and bold.
The blue Aegean girds this chosen home,
With ever-changing sound and light and foam,
Kissing the sifted sands, and caverns hoar;
And all the winds wandering along the shore
Undulate with the undulating tide:
There are thick woods where sylvan forms abide;
And many a fountain, rivulet, and pond,
As clear as elemental diamond,
Or serene morning air; and far beyond,
The mossy tracks made by the goats and deer
(Which the rough shepherd treads but once a year,)
Pierce into glades, caverns, and bowers, and halls
Built round with ivy, which the waterfalls

Illumining, with sound that never fails
Accompany the noonday nightingales;
And all the place is peopled with sweet airs;
The light clear element which the isle wears
Is heavy with the scent of lemon flowers,
Which floats like mist laden with unseen showers,
And falls upon the eyelids like faint sleep;
And from the moss violets and jonquils peep,
And dart their arrowy odor through the brain
Till you might faint with that delicious pain.
And every motion, odor, beam, and tone,
With that deep music is in unison:
Which is a soul within the soul—they seem
Like echoes of an antenatal dream—
It is an isle 'twixt Heaven, Air, Earth, and Sea,
Cradled, and hung in clear tranquility;
Bright as that wandering Eden Lucifer,
Washed by the soft blue Oceans of young air.
It is a favored place. Famine or Blight,
Pestilence, War and Earthquake, never light
Upon its mountain peaks; blind vultures, they
Sail onward far upon their fatal way:
The winged storms, chaunting their thunder psalm
To other lands, leave azure chasms of calm
Over this isle, or weep themselves in dew,
From which its fields and woods ever renew
Their green and golden immortality.
And from the sea there rise, and from the sky
There fall, clear exhalations, soft and bright,
Veil after veil, each hiding some delight,
Which Sun or Moon or zephyr draw aside,
Till the isle's beauty, like a naked bride
Glowing at once with love and loveliness,
Blushes and trembles at its own excess:
Yet, like a buried lamp, a Soul no less

Burns in the heart of this delicious isle,
An atom of th' Eternal, whose own smile
Unfolds itself, and may be felt not seen
O'er the gray rocks, blue waves, and forests green,
Filling their bare and void interstices—
But the chief marvel of the wilderness
Is a lone dwelling, built by whom or how
None of the rustic island people know:
'Tis not a tower of strength, though with its height
It overtops the woods; but, for delight,
Some wise and tender Ocean King, ere crime
Had been invented, in the world's young prime,
Reared it, a wonder of that simple time,
An envy of the isles, a pleasure house
Made sacred to his sister and his spouse.
It scarce seems now a wreck of human art,
But, as it were Titanic; in the heart
Of Earth having assumed its form, then grown
Out of the mountains, from the living stone,
Lifting itself in caverns light and high:
For all the antique and learned imagery
Has been erased, and in the place of it
The ivy and the wild vine interknit
The volumes of their many twining stems;
Parasite flowers illume with dewy gems
The lampless halls, and when they fade, the sky
Peeps through their winter woof of tracery
With Moonlight patches, or star atoms keen,
Or fragments of the day's intense serene—
Working mosaic on their Parian floors.
And, day and night, aloof, from the high towers
And terraces, the Earth and Ocean seem
To sleep in one another's arms, and dream
Of waves, flowers, clouds, woods, rocks, and all that we
Read in their smiles, and call reality.

This isle and house are mine, and I have vowed
Thee to be lady of the solitude—
And I have fitted up some chambers there
Looking towards the golden Eastern air,
And level with the living winds, which flow
Like waves above the living waves below—
I have sent books and music there, and all
Those instruments with which high spirits call
The future from its cradle, and the past
Out of its grave, and make the present last
In thoughts and joys which sleep, but cannot die,
Folded within their own eternity.
Our simple life wants little, and true taste
Hires not the pale drudge Luxury, to waste
The scene it would adorn, and therefore still,
Nature, with all her children, haunts the hill.
The ringdove, in the embowering ivy, yet
Keeps up her love lament, and the owls flit
Round the evening tower, and the young stars glance
Between the quick bats in their twilight dance;
The spotted deer bask in the fresh moonlight
Before our gate, and the slow, silent night
Is measured by the pants of their calm sleep.
Be this our home in life, and when years heap
Their withered hours, like leaves, on our decay,
Let us become the overhanging day,
The living soul of this Elysian isle,
Conscious, inseparable, one. Meanwhile
We two will rise, and sit, and walk together,
Under the roof of blue Ionian weather,
And wander in the meadows, or ascend
The mossy mountains, where the blue heavens bend
With lightest winds, to touch their paramour;
Or linger, where the pebble-paven shore,
Under the quick, faint kisses of the sea
Trembles and sparkles as with ecstasy—
Possessing and possessed by all that is

Within that calm circumference of bliss,
And by each other, till to love and live
Be one—or, at the noontide hour, arrive
Where some old cavern hoar seems yet to keep
The moonlight of the expired night asleep,
Through which the awakened day can never peep;
A veil for our seclusion, close as Night's,
Where secure sleep may kill thine innocent lights;
Sleep, the fresh dew of languid love, the rain
Whose drops quench kisses till they burn again.
And we will talk, until thought's melody
Become too sweet for utterance, and it die
In words, to live again in looks, which dart
With thrilling tone into the voiceless heart,
Harmonizing silence without a sound.
Our breath shall intermix, our bosoms bound,
And our veins beat together; and our lips
With other eloquence than words, eclipse
The soul that burns between them, and the wells
Which boil under our being's inmost cells,
The fountains of our deepest life, shall be
Confused in passion's golden purity,
As mountain springs under the morning Sun.
We shall become the same, we shall be one
Spirit within two frames, oh! wherefore two?
One passion in twin hearts, which grows and grew,
Till like two meteors of expanding flame,
Those spheres instinct with it become the same,
Touch, mingle, are transfigured; ever still
Burning, yet ever inconsumable:
In one another's substance finding food,
Like flames too pure and light and unimbued
To nourish their bright lives with baser prey,
Which point to Heaven and cannot pass away:
One hope within two wills, one will beneath
Two overshadowing minds, one life, one death,
One Heaven, one Hell, one immortality,

And one annihilation. Woe is me!
The winged words on which my soul would pierce
Into the height of love's rare Universe,
Are chains of lead around its flight of fire—
I pant, I sink, I tremble, I expire!

Weak Verses, go, kneel at your Sovereign's feet,
And say—"We are the masters of thy slave;
What wouldest thou with us and ours and thine?"
Then call your sisters from Oblivion's cave,
All singing loud: "Love's very pain is sweet,
But its reward is in the world divine
Which, if not here, it builds beyond the grave."
So shall we live when I am there. Then haste
Over the hearts of men, until ye meet
Marina, Vanna, Primus, and the rest,
And bid them love each other and be blest:
And leave the troop which errs, and which reproves,
And come and be my guest—for I am Love's.

Adonais

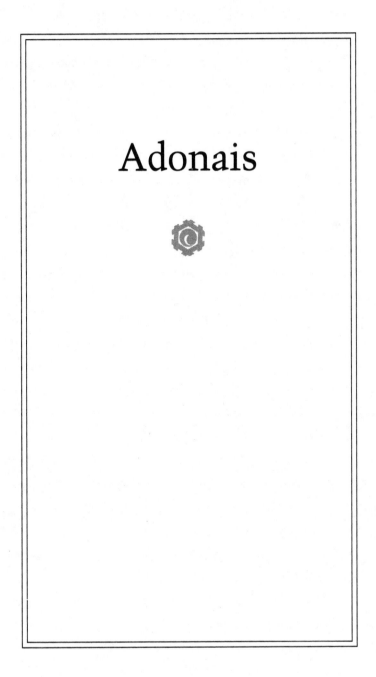

ADONAIS

An Elegy on the Death of John Keats, Author of Endymion, Hyperion, etc.

Preface

It is my intention to subjoin to the London edition of this poem, a criticism upon the claims of its lamented object to be classed among the writers of the highest genius who have adorned our age. My known repugnance to the narrow principles of taste on which several of his earlier compositions were modeled, prove, at least that I am an impartial judge. I consider the fragment of *Hyperion,* as second to nothing that was ever produced by a writer of the same years.

John Keats, died at Rome of a consumption, in his twenty-fourth year, on the —— of —— 1821; and was buried in the romantic and lonely cemetery of the protestants in that city, under the pyramid which is the tomb of Cestius, and the massy walls and towers, now moldering and desolate, which formed the circuit of ancient Rome. The cemetery is an open space among the ruins covered in winter with violets and daisies. It might make one in love with death, to think that one should be buried in so sweet a place.

The genius of the lamented person to whose memory I have dedicated these unworthy verses, was not less delicate and fragile than it was beautiful; and where cankerworms abound, what wonder if its young flower was blighted in the bud? The savage criticism on his *Endymion*, which appeared in the *Quarterly Review*, produced the most violent effect on his susceptible mind; the agitation thus originated ended in the rupture of a blood vessel in the lungs; a rapid consumption ensued, and the succeeding acknowledgments from more candid critics, of the true greatness of his powers, were ineffectual to heal the wound thus wantonly inflicted.

It may be well said, that these wretched men know not what they do. They scatter their insults and their slanders without heed as to whether the poisoned shaft lights on a heart made callous by many blows, or one, like Keats's composed of more penetrable stuff. One of their associates, is, to my knowledge, a most base and unprincipled calumniator. As to *Endymion*, was it a poem, whatever might be its defects, to be treated contemptuously by those who had celebrated, with various degrees of complacency and panegyric, *Paris*, and *Woman*, and a *Syrian Tale*, and Mrs. Lefanu, and Mr. Barrett, and Mr. Howard Payne, and a long list of the illustrious obscure? Are these the men, who in their venal good nature, presumed to draw a parallel between the Rev. Mr. Milman and Lord Byron? What gnat did they strain at here, after having swallowed all those camels? Against what woman taken in adultery, dares the foremost of these literary prostitutes to cast his opprobrious stone? Miserable man! you, one of the meanest, have wantonly defaced one of the noblest specimens of the workmanship of God. Nor shall it be your excuse, that, murderer as you are, you have spoken daggers, but used none.

The circumstances of the closing scene of poor Keats's life were not made known to me until the Elegy was ready for the press. I am given to understand that the wound which his sensitive spirit had received from the criticism of *Endymion,* was exasperated by the bitter sense of unrequited benefits; the poor fellow seems to have been hooted from the stage of life, no less by those on whom he had wasted the promise of his genius, than those on whom he had lavished his fortune and his care. He was accompanied to Rome, and attended in his last illness by Mr. Severn, a young artist of the highest promise, who, I have been informed "almost risked his own life, and sacrificed every prospect to unwearied attendance upon his dying friend." Had I known these circumstances before the completion of my poem, I should have been tempted to add my feeble tribute of applause to the more solid recompense which the virtuous man finds in the recollection of his own motives. Mr. Severn can dispense with a reward from "such stuff as dreams are made of." His conduct is a golden augury of the success of his future career—may the unextinguished Spirit of his illustrious friend animate the creations of his pencil, and plead against Oblivion for his name!

I

I weep for Adonais—he is dead!
O, weep for Adonais! though our tears
Thaw not the frost which binds so dear a head!
And thou, sad Hour, selected from all years
To mourn our loss, rouse thy obscure compeers,
And teach them thine own sorrow, say: with me
Died Adonais; till the Future dares
Forget the Past, his fate and fame shall be
An echo and a light unto eternity!

II

Where wert thou mighty Mother, when he lay,
When thy Son lay, pierced by the shaft which flies
In darkness? where was lorn Urania
When Adonais died? With veiled eyes,
'Mid listening Echoes, in her Paradise
She sate, while one, with soft enamored breath,
Rekindled all the fading melodies,
With which, like flowers that mock the corse beneath,
He had adorned and hid the coming bulk of death.

III

O, weep for Adonais—he is dead!
Wake, melancholy Mother, wake and weep!
Yet wherefore? Quench within their burning bed
Thy fiery tears, and let thy loud heart keep
Like his, a mute and uncomplaining sleep;
For he is gone, where all things wise and fair
Descend—oh, dream not that the amorous Deep
Will yet restore him to the vital air;
Death feeds on his mute voice, and laughs at our despair.

IV

Most musical of mourners, weep again!
Lament anew, Urania!—He died,
Who was the Sire of an immortal strain,
Blind, old, and lonely, when his country's pride,
The priest, the slave, and the liberticide,
Trampled and mocked with many a loathed rite
Of lust and blood; he went, unterrified,
Into the gulf of death; but his clear Sprite
Yet reigns o'er earth; the third among the sons of light.

V

Most musical of mourners, weep anew!
Not all to that bright station dared to climb;
And happier they their happiness who knew,
Whose tapers yet burn through that night of time
In which suns perished; others more sublime,
Struck by the envious wrath of man or God,
Have sunk, extinct in their refulgent prime;
And some yet live, treading the thorny road,
Which leads, through toil and hate, to Fame's serene
        abode.

VI

But now, thy youngest, dearest one, has perished
The nursling of thy widowhood, who grew,
Like a pale flower by some sad maiden cherished,
And fed with true love tears, instead of dew;
Most musical of mourners, weep anew!
Thy extreme hope, the loveliest and the last,
The bloom, whose petals nipped before they blew
Died on the promise of the fruit, is waste;
The broken lily lies—the storm is overpast.

VII

To that high Capital, where kingly Death
Keeps his pale court in beauty and decay,
He came; and bought, with price of purest breath,
A grave among the eternal—Come away!
Haste, while the vault of blue Italian day
Is yet his fitting charnel roof! while still
He lies, as if in dewy sleep he lay;
Awake him not! surely he takes his fill
Of deep and liquid rest, forgetful of all ill.

VIII

He will awake no more, oh, nevermore!—
Within the twilight chamber spreads apace,
The shadow of white Death, and at the door
Invisible Corruption waits to trace
His extreme way to her dim dwelling place;
The eternal Hunger sits, but pity and awe
Soothe her pale rage, nor dares she to deface
So fair a prey, till darkness, and the law
Of change, shall o'er his sleep the mortal curtain draw.

IX

O, weep for Adonais!—The quick Dreams,
The passion-winged Ministers of thought,
Who were his flocks, whom near the living streams
Of his young spirit he fed, and whom he taught
The love which was its music, wander not—
Wander no more, from kindling brain to brain,
But droop there, whence they sprung; and mourn
    their lot
Round the cold heart, where, after their sweet pain,
They ne'er will gather strength, or find a home again.

X

And one with trembling hands clasps his cold head,
And fans him with her moonlight wings, and cries;
"Our love, our hope, our sorrow, is not dead;
See, on the silken fringe of his faint eyes,
Like dew upon a sleeping flower, there lies
A tear some Dream has loosened from his brain."
Lost Angel of a ruined Paradise!
She knew not 'twas her own; as with no stain
She faded, like a cloud which had outwept its rain.

XI

One from a lucid urn of starry dew
Washed his light limbs as if embalming them;
Another clipped her profuse locks, and threw
The wreath upon him, like an anadem,
Which frozen tears instead of pearls begem;
Another in her willful grief would break
Her bow and winged reeds, as if to stem
A greater loss with one which was more weak;
And dull the barbed fire against his frozen cheek.

XII

Another Splendor on his mouth alit,
That mouth, whence it was wont to draw the breath
Which gave it strength to pierce the guarded wit,
And pass into the panting heart beneath
With lightning and with music: the damp death
Quenched its caress upon his icy lips;
And, as a dying meteor stains a wreath
Of moonlight vapor, which the cold night clips,
It flushed through his pale limbs, and past to its eclipse.

XIII

And others came . . . Desires and Adorations,
Winged Persuasions and veiled Destinies,
Splendors, and Glooms, and glimmering Incarnations
Of hopes and fears, and twilight Fantasies;
And Sorrow, with her family of Sighs,
And Pleasure, blind with tears, led by the gleam
Of her own dying smile instead of eyes,
Came in slow pomp—the moving pomp might seem
Like pageantry of mist on an autumnal stream.

XIV

All he had loved, and molded into thought,
From shape, and hue, and odor, and sweet sound,
Lamented Adonais. Morning sought
Her eastern watchtower, and her hair unbound,
Wet with the tears which should adorn the ground,
Dimmed the aerial eyes that kindle day;
Afar the melancholy thunder moaned,
Pale Ocean in unquiet slumber lay,
And the wild winds flew round, sobbing in their dismay.

XV

Lost Echo sits amid the voiceless mountains,
And feeds her grief with his remembered lay,
And will no more reply to winds or fountains,
Or amorous birds perched on the young green spray,
Or herdsman's horn, or bell at closing day;
Since she can mimic not his lips, more dear
Than those for whose disdain she pined away
Into a shadow of all sounds—a drear
Murmur, between their songs, is all the woodmen hear.

XVI

Grief made the young Spring wild, and she threw
    down
Her kindling buds, as if she Autumn were,
Or they dead leaves; since her delight is flown
For whom should she have waked the sullen year?
To Phoebus was not Hyacinth so dear
Nor to himself Narcissus, as to both
Thou Adonais: wan they stand and sere
Amid the faint companions of their youth,
With dew all turned to tears; odor, to sighing ruth.

XVII

Thy spirit's sister, the lorn nightingale
Mourns not her mate with such melodious pain;
Not so the eagle, who like thee could scale
Heaven, and could nourish in the sun's domain
Her mighty youth with morning, doth complain,
Soaring and screaming round her empty nest,
As Albion wails for thee: the curse of Cain
Light on his head who pierced thy innocent breast,
And scared the angel soul that was its earthly guest!

XVIII

Ah woe is me! Winter is come and gone,
But grief returns with the revolving year;
The airs and streams renew their joyous tone;
The ants, the bees, the swallows reappear;
Fresh leaves and flowers deck the dead Seasons' bier;
The amorous birds now pair in every brake,
And build their mossy homes in field and brere;
And the green lizard, and the golden snake,
Like unimprisoned flames, out of their trance awake.

XIX

Through wood and stream and field and hill and Ocean
A quickening life from the Earth's heart has burst
As it has ever done, with change and motion,
From the great morning of the world when first
God dawned on Chaos; in its steam immersed
The lamps of Heaven flash with a softer light;
All baser things pant with life's sacred thirst;
Diffuse themselves; and spend in love's delight,
The beauty and the joy of their renewed might.

XX

The leprous corpse touched by this spirit tender
Exhales itself in flowers of gentle breath;
Like incarnations of the stars, when splendor
Is changed to fragrance, they illumine death
And mock the merry worm that wakes beneath;
Naught we know, dies. Shall that alone which knows
Be as a sword consumed before the sheath
By sightless lightning?—th'intense atom glows
A moment, then is quenched in a most cold repose.

XXI

Alas! that all we loved of him should be,
But for our grief, as if it had not been,
And grief itself be mortal! Woe is me!
Whence are we, and why are we? of what scene
The actors or spectators? Great and mean
Meet massed in death, who lends what life must borrow.
As long as skies are blue, and fields are green,
Evening must usher night, night urge the morrow,
Month follow month with woe, and year wake year to
        sorrow.

XXII

He will awake no more, oh, nevermore!
"Wake thou," cried Misery, "childless Mother, rise
Out of thy sleep, and slake, in thy heart's core,
A wound more fierce than his with tears and sighs."
And all the Dreams that watched Urania's eyes,
And all the Echoes whom their sister's song
Had held in holy silence, cried: "Arise!"
Swift as a Thought by the snake Memory stung,
From her ambrosial rest the fading Splendor sprung.

XXIII

She rose like an autumnal Night, that springs
Out of the East, and follows wild and drear
The golden Day, which, on eternal wings,
Even as a ghost abandoning a bier,
Had left the Earth a corpse. Sorrow and fear
So struck, so roused, so rapt Urania;
So saddened round her like an atmosphere
Of stormy mist; so swept her on her way
Even to the mournful place where Adonais lay.

XXIV

Out of her secret Paradise she sped,
Through camps and cities rough with stone, and steel,
And human hearts, which to her aery tread
Yielding not, wounded the invisible
Palms of her tender feet where'er they fell:
And barbed tongues, and thoughts more sharp than
    they
Rent the soft Form they never could repel,
Whose sacred blood, like the young tears of May,
Paved with eternal flowers that undeserving way.

XXV

In the death chamber for a moment Death
Shamed by the presence of that living Might
Blushed to annihilation, and the breath
Revisited those lips, and life's pale light
Flashed through those limbs, so late her dear delight.
"Leave me not wild and drear and comfortless,
As silent lightning leaves the starless night!
Leave me not!" cried Urania: her distress
Roused Death: Death rose and smiled, and met her vain
      caress.

XXVI

"Stay yet awhile! speak to me once again;
Kiss me, so long but as a kiss may live;
And in my heartless breast and burning brain
That word, that kiss shall all thoughts else survive
With food of saddest memory kept alive,
Now thou art dead, as if it were a part
Of thee, my Adonais! I would give
All that I am to be as thou now art!
But I am chained to Time, and cannot thence depart!

XXVII

"Oh gentle child, beautiful as thou wert,
Why didst thou leave the trodden paths of men
Too soon, and with weak hands though mighty heart
Dare the unpastured dragon in his den?
Defenseless as thou wert, oh where was then
Wisdom the mirrored shield, or scorn the spear?
Or hadst thou waited the full cycle, when
Thy spirit should have filled its crescent sphere,
The monsters of life's waste had fled from thee like deer.

XXVIII

"The herded wolves, bold only to pursue;
The obscene ravens, clamorous o'er the dead;
The vultures to the conqueror's banner true
Who feed where Desolation first has fed,
And whose wings rain contagion—how they fled,
When like Apollo, from his golden bow,
The Pythian of the age one arrow sped
And smiled!—The spoilers tempt no second blow,
They fawn on the proud feet that spurn them lying low.

XXIX

"The sun comes forth, and many reptiles spawn;
He sets, and each ephemeral insect then
Is gathered into death without a dawn,
And the immortal stars awake again;
So is it in the world of living men:
A godlike mind soars forth, in its delight
Making earth bare and veiling heaven, and when
It sinks, the swarms that dimmed or shared its light
Leave to its kindred lamps the spirit's awful night."

XXX

Thus ceased she: and the mountain shepherds came
Their garlands sere, their magic mantles rent;
The Pilgrim of Eternity, whose fame
Over his living head like Heaven is bent,
An early but enduring monument,
Came, veiling all the lightnings of his song
In sorrow; from her wilds Ierne sent
The sweetest lyrist of her saddest wrong,
And love taught grief to fall like music from his tongue.

XXXI

Midst others of less note, came one frail Form,
A phantom among men; companionless
As the last cloud of an expiring storm
Whose thunder is its knell; he, as I guess,
Had gazed on Nature's naked loveliness,
Actaeon-like, and now he fled astray
With feeble steps o'er the world's wilderness,
And his own thoughts, along that rugged way,
Pursued, like raging hounds, their father and their prey.

XXXII

A pardlike Spirit beautiful and swift—
A Love in desolation masked—a Power
Girt round with weakness—it can scarce uplift
The weight of the superincumbent hour;
It is a dying lamp, a falling shower,
A breaking billow—even whilst we speak
Is it not broken? On the withering flower
The killing sun smiles brightly: on a cheek
The life can burn in blood, even while the heart may break.

XXXIII

His head was bound with pansies overblown,
And faded violets, white, and pied, and blue;
And a light spear topped with a cypress cone,
Round whose rude shaft dark ivy tresses grew
Yet dripping with the forest's noonday dew,
Vibrated, as the ever-beating heart
Shook the weak hand that grasped it; of that crew
He came the last, neglected and apart;
A herd-abandoned deer struck by the hunter's dart.

XXXIV

All stood aloof, and at his partial moan
Smiled through their tears; well knew that gentle band
Who in another's fate now wept his own;
As in the accents of an unknown land,
He sung new sorrow; sad Urania scanned
The Stranger's mien, and murmured: "who art thou?"
He answered not, but with a sudden hand
Made bare his branded and ensanguined brow,
Which was like Cain's or Christ's—Oh! that it should be so!

XXXV

What softer voice is hushed over the dead?
Athwart what brow is that dark mantle thrown?
What form leans sadly o'er the white deathbed,
In mockery of monumental stone,
The heavy heart heaving without a moan?
If it be He, who, gentlest of the wise,
Taught, soothed, loved, honored the departed one;
Let me not vex, with inharmonious sighs
The silence of that heart's accepted sacrifice.

XXXVI

Our Adonais has drunk poison—oh!
What deaf and viperous murderer could crown
Life's early cup with such a draught of woe?
The nameless worm would now itself disown:
It felt, yet could escape the magic tone
Whose prelude held all envy, hate, and wrong,
But what was howling in one breast alone,
Silent with expectation of the song,
Whose master's hand is cold, whose silver lyre unstrung.

XXXVII

Live thou, whose infamy is not thy fame!
Live! fear no heavier chastisement from me,
Thou noteless blot on a remembered name!
But be thyself, and know thyself to be!
And ever at thy season be thou free
To spill the venom when thy fangs o'erflow:
Remorse and Self-contempt shall cling to thee;
Hot Shame shall burn upon thy secret brow,
And like a beaten hound tremble thou shalt—as now.

XXXVIII

Nor let us weep that our delight is fled
Far from these carrion kites that scream below;
He wakes or sleeps with the enduring dead;
Thou canst not soar where he is sitting now—
Dust to the dust! but the pure spirit shall flow
Back to the burning fountain whence it came,
A portion of the Eternal, which must glow
Through time and change, unquenchably the same,
Whilst thy cold embers choke the sordid hearth of shame.

XXXIX

Peace, peace! he is not dead, he doth not sleep—
He hath awakened from the dream of life—
'Tis we, who lost in stormy visions, keep
With phantoms an unprofitable strife,
And in mad trance, strike with our spirit's knife
Invulnerable nothings—*We* decay
Like corpses in a charnel; fear and grief
Convulse us and consume us day by day,
And cold hopes swarm like worms within our living clay.

XL

He has outsoared the shadow of our night;
Envy and calumny and hate and pain,
And that unrest which men miscall delight,
Can touch him not and torture not again;
From the contagion of the world's slow stain
He is secure, and now can never mourn
A heart grown cold, a head grown gray in vain;
Nor, when the spirit's self has ceased to burn,
With sparkless ashes load an unlamented urn.

XLI

He lives, he wakes—'tis Death is dead, not he;
Mourn not for Adonais—Thou young Dawn
Turn all thy dew to splendor, for from thee
The spirit thou lamentest is not gone;
Ye caverns and ye forests, cease to moan!
Cease ye faint flowers and fountains, and thou Air
Which like a mourning veil thy scarf hadst thrown
O'er the abandoned Earth, now leave it bare
Even to the joyous stars which smile on its despair!

XLII

He is made one with Nature: there is heard
His voice in all her music, from the moan
Of thunder, to the song of night's sweet bird;
He is a presence to be felt and known
In darkness and in light, from herb and stone,
Spreading itself where'er that Power may move
Which has withdrawn his being to its own;
Which wields the world with never wearied love,
Sustains it from beneath, and kindles it above.

XLIII

He is a portion of the loveliness
Which once he made more lovely: he doth bear
His part, while the one Spirit's plastic stress
Sweeps through the dull dense world, compelling there,
All new successions to the forms they wear;
Torturing th'unwilling dross that checks its flight
To its own likeness, as each mass may bear;
And bursting in its beauty and its might
From trees and beasts and men into the Heaven's light.

XLIV

The splendors of the firmament of time
May be eclipsed, but are extinguished not;
Like stars to their appointed height they climb
And death is a low mist which cannot blot
The brightness it may veil. When lofty thought
Lifts a young heart above its mortal lair,
And love and life contend in it, for what
Shall be its earthly doom, the dead live there
And move like winds of light on dark and stormy air.

XLV

The inheritors of unfulfilled renown
Rose from their thrones, built beyond mortal thought,
Far in the Unapparent. Chatterton
Rose pale, his solemn agony had not
Yet faded from him; Sidney, as he fought
And as he fell and as he lived and loved
Sublimely mild, a Spirit without spot,
Arose; and Lucan, by his death approved:
Oblivion as they rose shrank like a thing reproved.

XLVI

And many more, whose names on Earth are dark
But whose transmitted effluence cannot die
So long as fire outlives the parent spark,
Rose, robed in dazzling immortality.
"Thou art become as one of us," they cry,
"It was for thee yon kingless sphere has long
Swung blind in unascended majesty,
Silent alone amid an Heaven of song.
Assume thy winged throne, thou Vesper of our throng!"

Who mourns for Adonais? oh come forth
Fond wretch! and know thyself and him aright.
Clasp with thy panting soul the pendulous Earth;
As from a center, dart thy spirit's light
Beyond all worlds, until its spacious might
Satiate the void circumference: then shrink
Even to a point within our day and night;
And keep thy heart light lest it make thee sink
When hope has kindled hope, and lured thee to the brink.

XLVIII

Or go to Rome, which is the sepulcher
O, not of him, but of our joy: 'tis naught
That ages, empires, and religions there
Lie buried in the ravage they have wrought;
For such as he can lend—they borrow not
Glory from those who made the world their prey;
And he is gathered to the kings of thought
Who waged contention with their time's decay,
And of the past are all that cannot pass away.

XLIX

Go thou to Rome—at once the Paradise,
The grave, the city, and the wilderness;
And where its wrecks like shattered mountains rise,
And flowering weeds, and fragrant copses dress
The bones of Desolation's nakedness
Pass, till the Spirit of the spot shall lead
Thy footsteps to a slope of green access
Where, like an infant's smile, over the dead,
A light of laughing flowers along the grass is spread.

L

And gray walls molder round, on which dull Time
Feeds, like slow fire upon a hoary brand;
And one keen pyramid with wedge sublime,
Pavilioning the dust of him who planned
This refuge for his memory, doth stand
Like flame transformed to marble; and beneath,
A field is spread, on which a newer band
Have pitched in Heaven's smile their camp of death
Welcoming him we lose with scarce extinguished breath.

LI

Here pause: these graves are all too young as yet
To have outgrown the sorrow which consigned
Its charge to each; and if the seal is set,
Here, on one fountain of a mourning mind,
Break it not thou! too surely shalt thou find
Thine own well full, if thou returnest home,
Of tears and gall. From the world's bitter wind
Seek shelter in the shadow of the tomb.
What Adonais is, why fear we to become?

LII

The One remains, the many change and pass;
Heaven's light forever shines, Earth's shadows fly;
Life, like a dome of many-colored glass,
Stains the white radiance of Eternity,
Until Death tramples it to fragments—Die,
If thou wouldst be with that which thou dost seek!
Follow where all is fled!—Rome's azure sky,
Flowers, ruins, statues, music, words, are weak
The glory they transfuse with fitting truth to speak.

LIII

Why linger, why turn back, why shrink, my Heart?
Thy hopes are gone before; from all things here
They have departed; thou shouldst now depart!
A light is past from the revolving year,
And man, and woman; and what still is dear
Attracts to crush, repels to make thee wither.
The soft sky smiles—the low wind whispers near:
'Tis Adonais calls! oh, hasten thither,
No more let Life divide what Death can join together.

LIV

That Light whose smile kindles the Universe,
That Beauty in which all things work and move,
That Benediction which the eclipsing Curse
Of birth can quench not, that sustaining Love
Which through the web of being blindly wove
By man and beast and earth and air and sea,
Burns bright or dim, as each are mirrors of
The fire for which all thirst; now beams on me,
Consuming the last clouds of cold mortality.

LV

The breath whose might I have invoked in song
Descends on me; my spirit's bark is driven,
Far from the shore, far from the trembling throng
Whose sails were never to the tempest given;
The massy earth and sphered skies are riven!
I am borne darkly, fearfully, afar:
Whilst burning through the inmost veil of Heaven,
The soul of Adonais, like a star,
Beacons from the abode where the Eternal are.

The Triumph
of Life

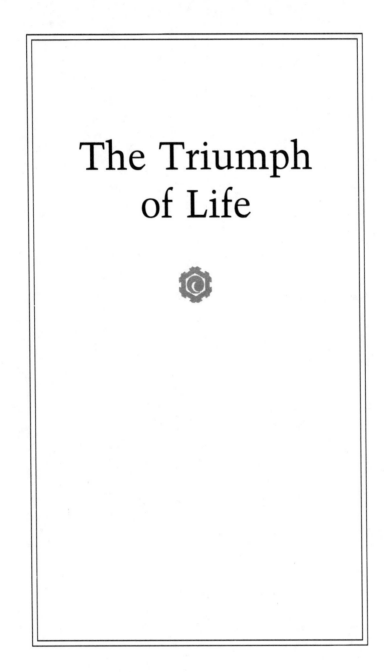

THE TRIUMPH OF LIFE

Swift as a spirit hastening to his task
  Of glory and of good, the Sun sprang forth
Rejoicing in his splendor, and the mask

  Of darkness fell from the awakened Earth.
The smokeless altars of the mountain snows
  Flamed above crimson clouds, and at the birth

Of light, the Ocean's orison arose
  To which the birds tempered their matin lay.
All flowers in field or forest which unclose

  Their trembling eyelids to the kiss of day,
Swinging their censers in the element,
  With orient incense lit by the new ray

Burned slow and inconsumably, and sent
  Their odorous sighs up to the smiling air,
And in succession due, did Continent,

  Isle, Ocean, and all things that in them wear
The form and character of mortal mold
  Rise as the Sun their father rose, to bear

Their portion of the toil which he of old
  Took as his own and then imposed on them;
But I, whom thoughts which must remain untold

  Had kept as wakeful as the stars that gem
The cone of night, now they were laid asleep,
  Stretched my faint limbs beneath the hoary stem

Which an old chestnut flung athwart the steep
    Of a green Apennine: before me fled
The night; behind me rose the day; the Deep

    Was at my feet, and Heaven above my head
When a strange trance over my fancy grew
    Which was not slumber, for the shade it spread

Was so transparent that the scene came through
    As clear as when a veil of light is drawn
O'er evening hills they glimmer; and I knew

    That I had felt the freshness of that dawn,
Bathed in the same cold dew my brow and hair
    And sate as thus upon that slope of lawn

Under the self same bough, and heard as there
    The birds, the fountains and the Ocean hold
Sweet talk in music through the enamored air.
    And then a Vision on my brain was rolled. . . .

As in that trance of wondrous thought I lay
    This was the tenor of my waking dream.
Methought I sate beside a public way

    Thick strewn with summer dust, and a great stream
Of people there was hurrying to and fro
    Numerous as gnats upon the evening gleam,

All hastening onward, yet none seemed to know
    Whither he went, or whence he came, or why
He made one of the multitude, yet so

Was borne amid the crowd as through the sky
One of the million leaves of summer's bier—
   Old age and youth, manhood and infancy,

Mixed in one mighty torrent did appear,
   Some flying from the thing they feared and some
Seeking the object of another's fear,

   And others as with steps towards the tomb
Pored on the trodden worms that crawled beneath,
   And others mournfully within the gloom

Of their own shadow walked, and called it death . . .
   And some fled from it as it were a ghost,
Half fainting in the affliction of vain breath.

   But more with motions which each other crossed
Pursued or shunned the shadows the clouds threw
   Or birds within the noonday ether lost,

Upon that path where flowers never grew;
   And weary with vain toil and faint for thirst
Heard not the fountains whose melodious dew

   Out of their mossy cells forever burst
Nor felt the breeze which from the forest told
   Of grassy paths, and wood lawns interspersed

With overarching elms and caverns cold,
   And violet banks where sweet dreams brood, but they
Pursued their serious folly as of old. . . .

   And as I gazed methought that in the way
The throng grew wilder, as the woods of June
   When the South wind shakes the extinguished day—

And a cold glare, intenser than the noon
    But icy cold, obscured with [   ] light
The Sun as he the stars. Like the young Moon

    When on the sunlit limits of the night
Her white shell trembles amid crimson air
    And whilst the sleeping tempest gathers might

Doth, as a herald of its coming, bear
    The ghost of her dead Mother, whose dim form
Bends in dark ether from her infant's chair,

    So came a chariot on the silent storm
Of its own rushing splendor, and a Shape
    So sate within as one whom years deform

Beneath a dusky hood and double cape
    Crouching within the shadow of a tomb,
And o'er what seemed the head a cloudlike crape

    Was bent, a dun and faint ethereal gloom
Tempering the light; upon the chariot's beam
    A Janus-visaged Shadow did assume

The guidance of that wonder-winged team.
    The Shapes which drew it in thick lightnings
Were lost: I heard alone on the air's soft stream

    The music of their ever moving wings.
All the four faces of that charioteer
    Had their eyes banded . . . little profit brings

Speed in the van and blindness in the rear,
    Nor then avail the beams that quench the Sun
Or that these banded eyes could pierce the sphere

Of all that is, has been, or will be done—
So ill was the car guided, but it past
　　With solemn speed majestically on . . .

The crowd gave way, and I arose aghast,
　　Or seemed to rise, so mighty was the trance,
And saw like clouds upon the thunder blast

　　The million with fierce song and maniac dance
Raging around; such seemed the jubilee
　　As when to greet some conqueror's advance

Imperial Rome poured forth her living sea
　　From senate house and prison and theater
When Freedom left those who upon the free

　　Had bound a yoke which soon they stooped to bear.
Nor wanted here the just similitude
　　Of a triumphal pageant, for where'er

The chariot rolled a captive multitude
　　Was driven; all those who had grown old in power
Or misery—all who have their age subdued,

　　By action or by suffering, and whose hour
Was drained to its last sand in weal or woe,
　　So that the trunk survived both fruit and flower;

All those whose fame or infamy must grow
　　Till the great winter lay the form and name
Of their own earth with them forever low—

　　All but the sacred few who could not tame
Their spirits to the Conqueror, but as soon
　　As they had touched the world with living flame

Fled back like eagles to their native noon,
    Or those who put aside the diadem
Of earthly thrones or gems, till the last one

    Were there; for they of Athens and Jerusalem
Were neither mid the mighty captives seen
    Nor mid the ribald crowd that followed them

Or fled before. . . . Swift, fierce and obscene
    The wild dance maddens in the van, and those
Who lead it, fleet as shadows on the green,

    Outspeed the chariot and without repose
Mix with each other in tempestuous measure
    To savage music. . . . Wilder as it grows,

They, tortured by the agonizing pleasure,
    Convulsed and on the rapid whirlwinds spun
Of that fierce spirit, whose unholy leisure

    Was soothed by mischief since the world begun,
Throw back their heads and loose their streaming hair,
    And in their dance round her who dims the Sun

Maidens and youths fling their wild arms in air
    As their feet twinkle; now recede and now
Bending within each other's atmosphere

    Kindle invisibly; and as they glow
Like moths by light attracted and repelled,
    Oft to new bright destruction come and go,

Till like two clouds into one vale impelled
    That shake the mountains when their lightnings mingle
And die in rain—the fiery band which held

Their natures, snaps . . . ere the shock cease to tingle
One falls and then another in the path
    Senseless, nor is the desolation single,

Yet ere I can say *where* the chariot hath
    Past over them; nor other trace I find
But as of foam after the Ocean's wrath

    Is spent upon the desert shore—Behind,
Old men, and women foully disarrayed
    Shake their gray hair in the insulting wind,

Limp in the dance and strain with limbs decayed
    To reach the car of light which leaves them still
Farther behind and deeper in the shade.

    But not the less with impotence of will
They wheel, though ghastly shadows interpose
    Round them and round each other, and fulfill

Their work and to the dust whence they arose
    Sink and corruption veils them as they lie—
And frost in these performs what fire in those.

    Struck to the heart by this sad pageantry,
Half to myself I said, "And what is this?
    Whose shape is that within the car? & why"—

I would have added—"is all here amiss?"
    But a voice answered . . . "Life" . . . I turned and knew
(O Heaven have mercy on such wretchedness!)

    That what I thought was an old root which grew
To strange distortion out of the hillside
    Was indeed one of that deluded crew,

And that the grass which methought hung so wide
    And white, was but his thin discolored hair,
And that the holes it vainly sought to hide

    Were or had been eyes—"If thou canst forbear
To join the dance, which I had well forborne,"
    Said the grim Feature, of my thought aware,

"I will tell all that which to this deep scorn
    Led me and my companions, and relate
The progress of the pageant since the morn;

    "If thirst of knowledge doth not thus abate,
Follow it even to the night, but I
    Am weary" . . . Then like one who with the weight

Of his own words is staggered, wearily
    He paused, and ere he could resume, I cried,
"First who art thou?" . . . "Before thy memory

    "I feared, loved, hated, suffered, did, and died,
And if the spark with which Heaven lit my spirit
    Earth had with purer nutriment supplied

"Corruption would not now thus much inherit
    Of what was once Rousseau—nor this disguise
Stain that within which still disdains to wear it—

    "If I have been extinguished, yet there rise
A thousand beacons from the spark I bore."—
    "And who are those chained to the car?" "The Wise,

"The great, the unforgotten: they who wore
    Miters and helms and crowns, or wreathes of light,
Signs of thought's empire over thought; their lore

"Taught them not this—to know themselves; their might
Could not repress the mutiny within,
   And for the morn of truth they reigned, deep night

"Caught them ere evening." "Who is he with chin
   Upon his breast and hands crossed on his chain?"
"The Child of a fierce hour; he sought to win

"The world, and lost all it did contain
Of greatness, in its hope destroyed; and more
   Of fame and peace than Virtue's self can gain

"Without the opportunity which bore
   Him on its eagle's pinion to the peak
From which a thousand climbers have before

"Fall'n as Napoleon fell."—I felt my cheek
Alter to see the great form pass away
   Whose grasp had left the giant world so weak

That every pygmy kicked it as it lay—
   And much I grieved to think how power and will
In opposition rule our mortal day—

And why God made irreconcilable
Good and the means of good; and for despair
   I half disdained mine eye's desire to fill

With the spent vision of the times that were
   And scarce have ceased to be . . . "Dost thou behold,"
Said then my guide, "those spoilers spoiled, Voltaire,

"Frederic, and Kant, Catherine, and Leopold,
Chained hoary anarchs, demagogue and sage
   Whose name the fresh world thinks already old—

"For in the battle Life and they did wage
    She remained conqueror—I was overcome
By my own heart alone, which neither age

    "Nor tears nor infamy nor now the tomb
Could temper to its object."—"Let them pass"—
    I cried—"the world and its mysterious doom

"Is not so much more glorious than it was
    That I desire to worship those who drew
New figures on its false and fragile glass

    "As the old faded."—"Figures ever new
Rise on the bubble, paint them how you may;
    We have but thrown, as those before us threw,

"Our shadows on it as it passed away.
    But mark, how chained to the triumphal chair
The mighty phantoms of an elder day—

    "All that is mortal of great Plato there
Expiates the joy and woe his master knew not;
    That star that ruled his doom was far too fair—

"And Life, where long that flower of Heaven grew not,
    Conquered the heart by love which gold or pain
Or age or sloth or slavery could subdue not

    "And near [   ] walk the [   ] twain.
The tutor and his pupil, whom Dominion
    Followed as tame as vulture in a chain—

"The world was darkened beneath either pinion
    Of him whom from the flock of conquerors
Fame singled as her thunderbearing minion;

— 240 —

"The other long outlived both woes and wars,
Throned in new thoughts of men, and still had kept
    The jealous keys of truth's eternal doors

"If Bacon's spirit [   ] had not leapt
    Like lightning out of darkness; he compelled
The Proteus shape of Nature's as it slept

"To wake and to unbar the caves that held
The treasure of the secrets of its reign—
    See the great bards of old who inly quelled

"The passions which they sung, as by their strain
    May well be known: their living melody
Tempers its own contagion to the vein

    "Of those who are infected with it—I
Have suffered what I wrote, or viler pain!—

    "And so my words were seeds of misery—
Even as the deeds of others."—"Not as theirs,"
    I said—he pointed to a company

In which I recognized amid the heirs
    Of Caesar's crime from him to Constantine.
The Anarchs old whose force and murderous snares

    Had rounded many a scepter bearing line
And spread the plague of blood and gold abroad,
    And Gregory and John and men divine

Who rose like shadows between Man and god
    Till that eclipse, still hanging under Heaven,
Was worshipped by the world o'er which they strode

For the true Sun it quenched—"Their power was given
But to destroy," replied the leader—"I
   Am one of those who have created, even

"If it be but a world of agony"—
   "Whence camest thou and whither goest thou?
How did thy course begin," I said, "and why?

   "Mine eyes are sick of this perpetual flow
Of people, and my heart of one sad thought—
   Speak." "Whence I came, partly I seem to know,

"And how and by what paths I have been brought
   To this dread pass, methinks even thou mayst guess;
Why this should be my mind can compass not;

   "Whither the conqueror hurries me still less.
But follow thou, and from spectator turn
   Actor or victim in this wretchedness,

"And what thou wouldst be taught I then may learn
   From thee—Now listen . . . In the April prime
When all the forest tops began to burn

   "With kindling green, touched by the azure clime
Of the young year, I found myself asleep
   Under a mountain, which from unknown time

"Had yawned into a cavern high and deep,
   And from it came a gentle rivulet
Whose water like clear air in its calm sweep

   "Bent the soft grass and kept forever wet
The stems of the sweet flowers, and filled the grove
   With sound which all who hear must needs forget

"All pleasure and all pain, all hate and love,
    Which they had known before that hour of rest:
A sleeping mother then would dream not of

"The only child who died upon her breast
At eventide, a king would mourn no more
    The crown of which his brow was dispossessed

"When the sun lingered o'er the Ocean floor
    To gild his rival's new prosperity—
Thou wouldst forget thus vainly to deplore

"Ills, which if ills, can find no cure from thee,
The thought of which no other sleep will quell
    Nor other music blot from memory—

"So sweet and deep is the oblivious spell—
    Whether my life had been before that sleep
The Heaven which I imagine, or a Hell

"Like this harsh world in which I wake to weep,
I know not. I arose and for a space
    The scene of woods and waters seemed to keep,

"Though it was now broad day, a gentle trace
    Of light diviner than the common Sun
Sheds on the common Earth, but all the place

"Was filled with many sounds woven into one
Oblivious melody, confusing sense
    Amid the gliding waves and shadows dun;

"And as I looked the bright omnipresence
    Of rooming through the orient cavern flowed,
And the Sun's image radiantly intense

"Burned on the waters of the well that glowed
Like gold, and threaded all the forest maze
    With winding paths of emerald fire—there stood

"Amid the sun, as he amid the blaze
    Of his own glory, on the vibrating
Floor of the fountain, paved with flashing rays,

    "A shape all light, which with one hand did fling
Dew on the earth, as if she were the Dawn
    Whose invisible rain forever seemed to sing

"A silver music on the mossy lawn,
    And still before her on the dusky grass
Iris her many colored scarf had drawn—

    "In her right hand she bore a crystal glass
Mantling with bright Nepenthe—the fierce splendor
    Fell from her as she moved under the mass

"Of the deep cavern, and with palms so tender
    Their tread broke not the mirror of its billow,
Glided along the river, and did bend her

    "Head under the dark boughs, till like a willow
Her fair hair swept the bosom of the stream
    That whispered with delight to be their pillow—

"As one enamored is upborne in dream
    O'er lily-paven lakes mid silver mist
To wondrous music, so this shape might seem

    "Partly to tread the waves with feet which kissed
The dancing foam, partly to glide along
    The airs that roughened the moist amethyst,

"Or the slant morning beams that fell among
  The trees, or the soft shadows of the trees;
And her feet ever to the ceaseless song

"Of leaves and winds and waves and birds and bees
And falling drops moved in a measure new
  Yet sweet, as on the summer evening breeze

"Up from the lake a shape of golden dew
  Between two rocks, athwart the rising moon,
Dances i' the wind where eagle never flew—

"And still her feet, no less than the sweet tune
To which they moved, seemed as they moved, to blot
  The thoughts of him who gazed on them, and soon

"All that was seemed as if it had been not,
  As if the gazer's mind was strewn beneath
Her feet like embers, and she, thought by thought,

"Trampled its fires into the dust of death,
As Day upon the threshold of the east
  Treads out the lamps of night, until the breath

"Of darkness reillumines even the least
  Of heaven's living eyes—like day she came,
Making the night a dream; and ere she ceased

"To move, as one between desire and shame
Suspended, I said—'If, as it doth seem,
  Thou comest from the realm without a name,

"'Into this valley of perpetual dream,
  Show whence I came, and where I am, and why—
Pass not away upon the passing stream.'

"'Arise and quench thy thirst,' was her reply.
And as a shut lily, stricken by the wand
  Of dewy morning's vital alchemy,

"I rose; and, bending at her sweet command,
  Touched with faint lips the cup she raised,
And suddenly my brain became as sand

  "Where the first wave had more than half erased
The track of deer on desert Labrador,
  Whilst the fierce wolf from which they fled amazed

"Leaves his stamp visibly upon the shore
  Until the second bursts—so on my sight
Burst a new Vision never seen before—

  "And the fair shape waned in the coming light
As veil by veil the silent splendor drops
  From Lucifer, amid the chrysolite

"Of sunrise ere it strike the mountaintops—
  And as the presence of that fairest planet
Although unseen is felt by one who hopes

  "That his day's path may end as he began it
In that star's smile, whose light is like the scent
  Of a jonquil when evening breezes fan it,

"Or the soft notes in which his dear lament
  The Brescian shepherd breathes, or the caress
That turned his weary slumber to content—

  "So knew I in that light's severe excess
The presence of that shape which on the stream
  Moved, as I moved along the wilderness,

"More dimly than a day appearing dream,
  The ghost of a forgotten form of sleep,
A light from Heaven whose half extinguished beam

"Through the sick day in which we wake to weep
Glimmers, forever sought, forever lost—
  So did that shape its obscure tenor keep

"Beside my path, as silent as a ghost;
  But the new Vision, and its cold bright car,
With savage music, stunning music, crossed

"The forest, and as if from some dread war
Triumphantly returning, the loud million
  Fiercely extolled the fortune of her star—

"A moving arch of victory the vermilion
  And green and azure plumes of Iris had
Built high over her wind-winged pavilion,

"And underneath ethereal glory clad
The wilderness, and far before her flew
  The tempest of the splendor which forbade

"Shadow to fall from leaf or stone—the crew
  Seemed in that light like atomies that dance
Within a sunbeam—Some upon the new

"Embroidery of flowers that did enhance
The grassy vesture of the desert, played,
  Forgetful of the chariot's swift advance;

"Others stood gazing till within the shade
  Of the great mountain its light left them dim—
Others outspeeded it, and others made

"Circles around it like the clouds that swim
Round the high moon in a bright sea of air,
 And more did follow, with exulting hymn,

"The chariot and the captives fettered there,
 But all like bubbles on an eddying flood
Fell into the same track at last and were

 "Borne onward—I among the multitude
Was swept; me sweetest flowers delayed not long,
 Me not the shadow nor the solitude,

"Me not the falling stream's Lethean song,
 Me, not the phantom of that early form
Which moved upon its motion—but among

 "The thickest billows of the living storm
I plunged, and bared my bosom to the clime
 Of that cold light, whose airs too soon deform—

"Before the chariot had begun to climb
 The opposing steep of that mysterious dell,
Behold a wonder worthy of the rhyme

 "Of him who from the lowest depths of Hell
Through every Paradise and through all glory
 Love led serene, and who returned to tell

"In words of hate and awe the wondrous story
 How all things are transfigured, except Love;
For deaf as is a sea which wrath makes hoary

 "The world can hear not the sweet notes that move
The sphere whose light is melody to lovers—
 A wonder worthy of his rhyme—the grove

"Grew dense with shadows to its inmost covers,
    The earth was gray with phantoms, and the air
Was peopled with dim forms, as when there hovers

    "A flock of vampire bats before the glare
Of the tropic sun, bringing ere evening
    Strange night upon some Indian isle—thus were

"Phantoms diffused around, and some did fling
    Shadows of shadows, yet unlike themselves,
Behind them, some like eaglets on the wing

    "Were lost in the white blaze, others like elves
Danced in a thousand unimagined shapes
    Upon the sunny streams and grassy shelves;

"And others sate chattering like restless apes
    On vulgar paws and voluble like fire.
Some made a cradle of the ermined capes

    "Of kingly mantles, some upon the tiar
Of pontiffs sate like vultures, others played
    Within the crown which girt with empire

"A baby's or an idiot's brow, and made
    Their nests in it; the old anatomies
Sate hatching their bare brood under the shade

    "Of demon wings, and laughed from their dead eyes
To reassume the delegated power
    Arrayed in which these worms did monarchize

"Who make this earth their charnel—Others more
    Humble, like falcons sate upon the fist
Of common men, and round their heads did soar,

"Or like small gnats and flies, as thick as mist
On evening marshes, thronged about the brow
    Of lawyer, statesman, priest and theorist,

"And others like discolored flakes of snow
    On fairest bosoms and the sunniest hair
Fell, and were melted by the youthful glow

"Which they extinguished; for like tears, they were
A veil to those from whose faint lids they rained
    In drops of sorrow—I became aware

"Of whence those forms proceeded which thus stained
    The track in which we moved; after brief space
From every form the beauty slowly waned,

"From every firmest limb and fairest face
The strength and freshness fell like dust, and left
    The action and the shape without the grace

"Of life; the marble brow of youth was cleft
    With care, and in the eyes where once hope shone
Desire like a lioness bereft

"Of its last cub, glared ere it died; each one
Of that great crowd sent forth incessantly
    These shadows, numerous as the dead leaves blown

"In Autumn evening from a poplar tree—
    Each, like himself and like each other were,
At first, but soon distorted, seemed to be

"Obscure clouds molded by the casual air;
And of this stuff the car's creative ray
    Wrought all the busy phantoms that were there

"As the sun shapes the clouds—thus, on the way
    Mask after mask fell from the countenance
And form of all, and long before the day

    "Was old, the joy which waked like Heaven's glance
The sleepers in the oblivious valley, died,
    And some grew weary of the ghastly dance

"And fell, as I have fallen by the wayside,
    Those soonest from whose forms most shadows past
And least of strength and beauty did abide."—

    "Then, what is Life?" I said . . . the cripple cast
His eye upon the car which now had rolled
    Onward, as if that look must be the last,

And answered. . . ."Happy those for whom the fold
    Of

INDEX OF TITLES AND FIRST LINES